NICE, RUM AN' COCA COLA and **WEL(**

Mustapha Matura is 'the most perceptive a
writing in Britain' (Benedict Nightingale, *I*
volume, published alongside the opening o
Matura's recent work.

Nice is a funny, deeply ironic monologue for a black man recently arrived in
Britain and touchingly anxious to please. In **Rum an' C**oca Cola, set on a beach in
Trinidad, two beguiling buskers are trying to complete a song for the annual
calypso competition. These gentle beginnings belie the play's bloody end, but not
its 'wit, feeling and invention, the qualities that continue to distinguish Mr
Matura's writing' (Robert Cushman, *Observer*). **Welcome Home Jacko,** 'A jack-
knife of a play' (*Guardian*), is set in a London youth club. 'There's reggae music
on the record player, concert posters and LP covers on the walls, and four West
Indian boys in flashy hats playing table football as if their lives depended on it. But
the fun turns sour with two arrivals from the real world . . . It is a concise,
intelligent, often hilarious, eventually sad play which shows Mustapha Matura at
the top of his form' (Christopher Hudson, *Evening Standard*).

NICE
RUM AN' COCA COLA
&
WELCOME HOME JACKO

Three Plays by

MUSTAPHA MATURA

A Methuen New Theatrescript
Eyre Methuen · London

First published in 1980 by Eyre Methuen Ltd, 11 New Fetter Lane,
London EC4P 4EE
Copyright © 1980 by Mustapha Matura

ISBN 0 413 47720 7 – ï

NICE

A Monologue

Nice was first staged at The Almost Free Theatre, London, on 12 February 1973, with Stefan Kalipha as the MAN. The production was directed by the author. It was subsequently revived at Riverside Studios, Hammersmith, on 5 January 1980, with Norman Beaton, and was again directed by Mustapha Matura.

A prison canteen (tables, chairs etc). In it a black man in uniform. He is thirty-five to forty years old. He is sweeping/wiping and speaks directly to the audience.

MAN: Wen a come off de boat de customs man was nice ter me, so i was nice back ter him, but a friend a mine who come ter meet me say, boy yer shouldn't be nice ter dem, dey do' like we, but i say nar man it en so, so at all, wen people nice ter yer, you must be nice back ter dem, an if yer want people ter be nice ter you, you must be nice ter dem, but anyhow he say a was foolish an a go fine out, but a was nice ter he so de next day he carry me down ter de exchange dey call it, and de man dey was nice ter me too, so a was nice back ter him, so wen dey give me dis job sweeping out a office, i say tank you ter de man, an he say tank you back ter me, but me friend say, a shouldn't say tank you ter him, but i say de man say tank you ter me so i say tank you back ter him, an i tell him if yer want people ter say tank you ter you you have ter say tank you ter dem, but he say how a was wrong, but i say nar man, i en wrong i rite, den he say how i stupid, but anyhow a say tank you ter him, so de next night he carry me ter a night club, where dey had some girls dancing wit coloured men, de first time a see white woman dance wit coloured man, and dey en dancing straight an back yer no, dey dancing wit dey bottom all over de place, so i say boy dis is de place fer me, so a went up an ask one a de girls nice fer a dance an she dance wit me an it was a good dance an we had a good time, but me friend pull me aside an say boy, how a go teach yer ter live in dis country wen yer do' listen ter me, yer mustn't be nice ter dem, dey do' want yer ter be nice ter dem, but i say nar man, dat en true because i was nice ter she an she was nice back ter me, but he say de same ting again dat i go fine out, so a miss a dance trying ter fine out, but a en fine out notting, so a went back an ask she ter dance an she say yes an we dance again, but a notice me friend wasn't dancing at all, so a say he must be en feel like dancing or maybe he foot hurting him, so anyhow wen de club start ter close me friend come pulling me saying le we go, le we go, but i say nar man, i go ask de lady ter go home wit she an see wha she say, but me friend say dey do' want we in de house much less in dey bed, he say dey only like ter dance wit we an get hot ter go an heat up de white boys, but i say nar man, dat en true, because i no dat if you heat up someting is you have ter eat it but he say i en no dese woman an i en go get notting off she an dat if a go wit she, in de morning she go cry out an say a hypnotise she an rape she, but i say nar man, it en so if a woman heat you up she heat you up fer a reason, an de reason is because she want you ter burn she, but he say i is a idiot an a go fine out but anyhow a ask she nicely ter come home wit she an she say yes, so a leave me friend outside de club, an me an she went home an had a nice time an in de morning she en cry out an bawl rape or anyting she just say she have ter go ter work an if a does go ter de club often, she go see me again, so i say yes a does go sometimes an a hope a go see she again, an she say she hope so too, so a went outside an a did'nt even no where a was but a ask a policeman nice an he tell me how ter catch a bus back ter me friend's house, boy wen a tell me friend wha happen yer shoulda see de man, de man went mad, de man start ter cuss me an call me all kinda names an tell me a shouldn't ask no policeman notting dat if yer ask dem anyting an dey fine out yer new dey go lock yer up fer someting, but i say nar man, if yer want ter fine out anyting is a policeman ter ask an if yer ask dem nice dey go answer yer back nice but he say a go fine out, but i say how a go fine out he just say a go fine out, but anyhow a was nice ter him so he take me ter de pub wit him, so wen we get inside de pub, i say le me buy de drinks, he say no, a mustn't buy drinks fer people, a must le dem buy de own drinks if a buy drinks fer dem dey go tink a stupid an drink up all me money, but i say nar man, it en so, if yer buy people drink dey go buy yer back a drink, but he say de same ting again how a foolish an how a go fine out, an if a don't hear a go feel, so anyhow dey had a white man stanning up next ter me so a buy him a drink an he buy me back a drink, so a say well if he buy me back a drink, a have ter buy he back a drink an so it go on until me friend say yer see wha a tell yer de man go drink out all yer money but i say nar man, dat en go happen, but anyhow he say he going next door ter de betting shop an wen a ready ter go come fer him, so wen time come fer de pub ter close de white man a tink he name was Fred, Fred tell me he have a bet ter put on, dat he get some tip from some horse's mouth an if a have any money ter put it on it, so we went next door an put on de bet, a notice me friend wasn't looking too happy, so a say wha wrong man, he say he lost all he money, so i say well, look de man just give me a tip an he say ter put all yer money on it, but he say dey en go give no coloured man horse ter back on, because dey en want ter see no coloured man win money, so i say nar man, because he just put he own money on it, but he say da is a trick ter fool me, but i say he fool he self because he put more money dan me, anyhow de horse come twenty ter one so i en do bad at all anyhow a give me friend a five pound note an we went home wen we get dey who could be waiting fer we but de girl from de club, de same girl a meet last night, she say how she pass in ter see if a was going ter de club later, a musta tell she where a was living, but i say well if yer going ter de club ter night yer might as well stay here an wen time come fer we ter go we could go together so she come inside an me friend say dat if people see she come after work dey go say dat she working fer me, but i say nar man, dey car say dat, i only meet she last night how dey go say dat, but he say a go fine out an dat he going an see a film round de corner, now dat surprise me because i no he wasn't no theatre man, but a say he must be feeling lonely so anyhow de girl take off she shoes an start ter clean up de place, an wen she done she say wha we have ter eat, i tell she notting, she say not ter worry dat she go go round de corner and get someting, so i say da is awright wit me, so she went, wen she come back de woman cook one food, pardner a never no white woman could cook so, so a say dat dis woman is someting boy, an den after we finish eat she take off all she clothes an say she want de same dat a give she last night, so i say awright an a give she it an we had a nice time man, wen time come fer we ter go ter de club, she say she tired so i say well le we stay here so she say right she is awright wit she, so da is how we spend de night, i en even no wat time me friend come in, wen he come in i en even hear im a just feel im trying ter pull de girl in he half a de bed, but she musta be too heavy fer he, because he give up quick, but in de morning a went ter work an leave she dey wit him so i en no wha

happen wen a come back home de night an tell de man wat a nice foreman a had yer shoulda see de man go mad, just like wid de policeman so ter change de subject, a ask him wha bout de girl if she get out awright he say yes but a shouldn't tink de foreman nice because dey en nice an dat he job is ter make coloured people work hard, but i say nar man, dat en true dem have ter work hard too, but he say is a different kinda work, but i say work is work an if yer working someplace wit people yer have ter be nice wit dem, but he say how a go learn, an how de girl leave a message saying how she go be at de club ter night an dat i must come, so a tell im tank yer, but boy a was feeling so tired i say i en going ter no club ternight he say, yer see how tired yer is, is because de foreman working yer hard, but i no a was tired fer someting else, but he say it was de foreman so i en say notting, anyhow bout twelve a clock de door bell start ter ring, who it could be but de girl, de same girl from de club, de girl who come home here an cook me a meal, she say she en see me in de club an she come ter see if anyting wrong wit me, but i say nar man, nottin en wrong i just taking a rest da is all, so a ask she if she want ter come in an stay, but she an me friend say de same ting, she say she en want ter stay, an me friend say he en want she ter stay, so a figure dey musta have a row or someting anyhow a put on me clothes an went round by she an we had a good time again, wen a come back from work dat night, me friend say boy, wha yer doing de woman go kill yer, i say nar man, she en go kill me, den he say dem white woman could take more man dan we no, so den i ask him how he go feel, if a move out because is me an he was paying de rent, well boy de man went mad again, just like wit de policeman, an wit de foreman, he start ter cuss me an say how a ungrateful, an how is he who look after me wen a first come ter dis country, an my people beg him ter look out ter fer me, an how now i want ter left him in a lurch, boy a never see a man go so crazy, an den he ask me if a moving in wit de girl, so i tell im a wasn't sure as yet but a was tinking of it, well is den he start ter cuss me, an buse me, well boy wha a could do, but say tank yer fer looking after me but i en want yer ter look after me no more, an a go pack up an leave by ter night, but yer see deep down inside i no he was a nice guy, because he en charge me no rent fer de four days a stay by he, anyhow a move in wit dis girl, well it was awright wen we first start, but den de woman start ter do all kinda a ting like tell me how a mustn't wear sock in bed, i tell she a cole, an how a mustn't wear me pajamas under me clothes, again a tell she it cole, but like she en hear an how i mustn't be nice ter de woman next door, an one set a i must do dis an i mustn't do dis, so i tell she nar man, dat en go happen because fer one ting wen it a cole me en want ter take off no pajamas is den yer go catch cole, but she en listen, she tell me i stupid an i en no bout dis country, an dat de woman next door go believe i after someting because i so nice ter her, but i tell she nar man it en so, is wen yer nice ter people dey go be nice ter you, but den she come like me friend she call me idiot an burke a was going an tell she me name wasn't burke but a was too tired, so anyhow one day wen a come home from work, just as a reach de top a de stairs, who should come outa she door but de woman from next door, so i give she a howdy like a does do anytime a does see she, anyhow dis time she ask me if a have a shilling fer de meter, well a tell she i en have no shilling on me but a have one inside on de mantlepiece, she say go in fer it, so i say awright, an a open de door, soon as de woman come in de room, de woman start ter get on, de woman start ter tell me all kinda ting like how i so nice an she like me because i so nice, so i tell she i tink she nice too, an yer no wat de next ting a no is me an de woman having a nice time on de bed, den de woman start ter bawl an groan like she never want ter stop, so me en stop she, de next ting a no is de door bust open an who should come in but, de girl who a living wit, de same girl from de club, well boy a never jump so fast, but it en me she go fer is de woman next door, both a dem start ter cuss one another an row a never no white woman could cuss so much, de girl tell de woman how she is a hoe, an de woman tell de girl how she is a slut, an how she wouldn't push me wit a barge pole, an how is me who pull she in de room an give she a asprin an take advantage a she headache, so boy yer could imagine de fix a in, so right dere an den a say de best ting ter do is go, so whilst both a dem rowing a pick up me bag an

put me clothes in it, an as a hit de door, de girl turn round an notice a going, she say wha yer going, a say a going an stay wit me friend, boy de girl start ter cry an break down an tell me all kinda ting like how she love me an she car live witout me an how if a left she go kill she self, well boy dat slow me down, but is wen she tell me she go do anyting fer me den a stop, well by den de woman from next door gone, after a tell she tank you fer coming in, an she tell me tanks fer de shilling, so den de girl tell me how she go look after me an make sure i en have ter go ter work because she no i en like ter go ter work in de cole, well she was right dey, an another ting is she say she go bring enough money fer both a we, well boy wha a could say ter dat, a tell she tanks dat da is awright wit me, an she say awright too as long as a do' leave, well a put down me bag an is den she start ter tell me how she love me an how no man ever please she like how i please she, so anyhow tings start ter go good a went in an tell de foreman tank you fer de job an how a go be leaving soon an he say well how he go miss me an how it was nice having me work fer him, an ting, so pardner tings start ter get good de girl start ter work so hard dat after a while a never get ter see she, she go out ter work an wen she come back she sleep, but i didn't mind so much because everytime she come in she used ter bring in one set a five pound notes a never see so much money in me life, boy a tell yer i'd go outside an spend an spend an de money still wouldn't done, so after awhile a start ter save it, anyhow a didn't mind not seeing she so much because de woman from next door used ter cook me food an bring it in an me an she use ter have a good time, so a couldn't complain too much, now de next ting a no is she too say she want ter go out an work fer me because she could do better dan de girl, an how she have more contacts an she could work harder, so i say awright den give it a try no harm in trying an see if yer like it, so anyhow she look happy wen a tell she dat, but de only ting was worrying me is who go cook me food, because wit both a dem out a go starve, but anyhow a say well if tings turn out so wha a go do, but as soon as a say dat wat should happen but a knock on de door, an who it could be but de landlady she say she come ter collect some rent, so i tell she ter hold on a minute an le me open de door well she come in de room ter collect she rent but i feel she come in ter look around, so i en say notting because is she place an if she want ter look around an see wha going on she have a right ter do dat, anyhow we sit down talking an de next ting a no is how she start ter tell me bout she husband an how bad he does treat she an how he do give she notting so i say well some man like dat an she say how i nice an how i understand an how she feel she could talk ter me, so i say tank you because if people feel dey could talk ter you dey must be like you, so boy we sit down dey talking, all morning an den she say well is lunch time an she have ter go down an cook an how nice it was talking ter me an she sorry how she take up all me time, but i tell she nar man, it en so is awright i enjoy it so den she say how she go make up fer it by bringing some lunch fer me so i say awright den if da is wat yer want ter do, do nottin else, so anyhow she bring up de lunch and a must say she cooking was'nt so hot but i tell she i taste nice an she like dat because de next ting she do is ter give me a hug an a kiss, so i say well if yer want ter give me a hug an kiss, i want ter give you a hug an kiss too, well she say she would like dat because is a long time no man hug she an kiss she, not because no man en want ter do it but because she en want any kinda man ter do it, de man she want ter do it must be a nice man, an he must be a kind man an he must understand she well i tell she she right ter want dat an anyhow me an she had a good time man, everyday she used ter cook me food an come up an me an she would have a good time until she husband come home from work den a wouldn't see she but a would no she was dey because sometimes she would start singing, i love you baby, an i need you baby, an sometimes she would collect de rent in de morning an put it back under de door in de evening, so i no she was dere, anyhow one day me an she husband was talking an he say how dat he always wanted ter go ter de West Indies because de people always so happy an nice so i tell im dat if he tink de people so nice over here he should go down dere an he go see how nice dey really is an i even tell him how if he go down dere he could stay with my people an dem an he say how nice dat was an tank me an ting, so after dat me an he was de best a friend an he

used ter ask me tings like he hope he wife singing do' bodder me an i no how woman was, i say nar man, i do' mind i like she singing an i glad ter hear people singing, because wen dey do dat it mean dey happy, an i like ter no people happy, an is a funny ting because den he used ter get serious but den he would start smiling again, so he was awright an yer no someting he never used ter take me ter he pub but everytime he come back he used ter bring me a guinness, yer could beat dat everytime like de sun rise, but a never fine out wha he used ter mean by do kill meself guinness car kill, but anyhow he was me mate, de first mate a ever had, anyhow yer see how some people could be nice, so one day a buy one a dem jaguar cars an who a should see crossing de road in front a me, right cross me bonnet but me friend, me same friend who meet me off de boat, so i say wha happening man, how life treating yer, he say not bad he still trying he luck wit de horses an dem but it look like i doing awright, so i say nar man, it might look so but i still paying rent an dat en so good, but he say well a look like a doing better dan he, so a telling im he must be backing de wrong horses, a taught i'd give him a joke an cheer him up yer no, but anyhow he en get no happier so a say i'd buy him a drink like old times, anyhow dat brighten him up a bit, so we went in a pub, wen we get inside de pub, de man start ter tell me he troubles how he was living wit some woman an how de woman take all he clothes an sell dem, an how he en have no money an no where ter live, so i say well boy yer could come an stay by me till tings get fer de better an he fine somewhere of he own, well is den he get bright because de next ting a no is he en finish he beer, de first time a ever see him en finish a whole beer, but anyhow we go home by he an pick up he few tings an a take him round by me, but it hit me dat my girl en like him, so she en go want him sleeping wit we so wha a go do, anyhow a no de landlady had a room going spare so a wasn't worried, anyhow wen a get dey a call she aside an explain de position ter she an she say is awright if is a friend a mine, but boy some people de more yer do ter help dem is de more dey let yer down, no sooner dan de man get in de house de man want ter no where all de meters is an wha kinda locks dey have on dem, yer could beat dat, so i say well look man, yer get a room, yer get a food, well take it easy, rest yer body an see how tings go ner, but nar, he say i soft, i en have no brains, i car see further dan me eye, an i en have no business brains, so i say well if is meter yer looking ter teef from he en have no brains, because if yer teef dey go lock yer up, so better dan dey lock yer up, here look some money from me wen yer get a job pay me back, well boy if yer see de man grab de money, no sooner a take de money out me pocket, it was in he hand, so he was awright but de next ting a no is he trying ter pull de landlady in he room, one night de same one who does sing i love you baby, an i need you baby, she say she en give im no cause ter pull she in he room, but i en so sure, yer do no how people does take tings, a mean ter say he hear she singing i love you baby, i need you baby, he must be tink is he she talking bout, yer car blame de guy, so i say well look if is woman yer want why yer do ask dem nice ter give yer a piece he say he do ask no woman fer notten an he en asking no woman fer notten wat he want he go take an wen he want a woman he go take she, so i say look pardner it en so it go, dat if he ask he never ter no he might get it, but anyhow he en listen, so de next ting a hear is he go in de woman next ter me room an smelling up all she panties, so i see him an a say ter him look ner man, if is a woman yer want ask me an a go get one fer yer, he say he en want no woman, woman is trouble, now dat start me tinkin because one minute he pulling de landlady in he room an de next he saying he en want no woman so wha he up to, so i say well look here i go give yer some money go an look fer yer own place de man start ter cry an beg me ter let him stay saying i is de only friend he ever had an how i treat him so good an how he shame he try ter take advantage a he position wit me, so i say nar man da is awright, as long as yer behave yer self an he say he go do dat so da was awright yer no wat happen, yer no wat de man do wen a tell yer some man bad dey bad yer no, de man go down stairs an tell de landlady husband how i an she carrying on but he en no i an he was mate so he come an tell me an we had a good laugh, but he en satisfy wit dat he go an tell de police how i living off prostitute not one but two prostitute, an i living off de immoral earnings, well anyhow wen de police come ter see me, de police start ter

laugh because he car see how a guy like me could have not one but two woman on de road fer him an he sorry dat he had ter trouble me so much, so i say a sorry dat he had trouble too, because wen people nice ter you, you must be nice back ter dem, so de police leave but de man en satisfy wit dat yer no wha he do, i en no where he get de letter form from, he write me modder an de woman a was living wit back home an tell dem, wait fer it, he tell dem how, boy some man malicious yer now, he tell dem how i doing well an how i making a lot a money, an how i have me own house an ting, well de next ting is dey write me after all yer car blame dem dey hear dey boy making money so dey bound ter write, well anyhow dey write me an say how as a doing so well if a could send fer dem, well wha a go do a say awright, as man, a have ter send fer dem, after all, a mean ter say so anyhow a went round de corner an buy a house, an a send fer dem, so all a dem come me modder de woman a was living wit an me four children, Clarice, Claudine, Clarissa an' Claude, move in ter de house round de corner, a used ter sleep dey nights an tell dem a had work ter do at de other house, so tings start ter go good, me modder start ter do some cleaning an me woman start ter take in some washing an make some plans ter open she own laundrette, so who could complain, but boy wen a tell yer dis life funny it funny yer no so tings start ter go good, wen de next ting a hear is me friend want ter see me so i say awright, but he round de corner, yer no, an he en a three penny bus ride away, nar man de man in Brixton Prison, so a get me forms ter visit wen a get dey, de first ting de man say is how a doing, so i say yer bring me all dis way ter ask me how a doing, but he say nar man, dat en wat he want ter see me for, he say he want me ter pay a fine fer him, so i say well da is awright, how much it is, well he say is only twenty pounds, it turn out he break a meter an dey charge im twenty pounds an he couldn't pay so dey trow him inside, so i pay de fine an dey let im out, but dat en all de man want me find place fer him ter live, so i say awright, a go do dat a figure prison must a change him, put some sense in him, so a give im a room in de house me modder an dem was living in, a figure me modder could keep a eye on him during de day an i could watch im during de night, an a tell im, a say if a only catch yer near me meter, is out yer going, friend or no friend, but he say nar man, dat en go happen, he change, he en go do dat kinda ting again, how he could do a ting lik dat ter me after a so nice ter him, an how if people nice ter yer yer must be nice ter dem, so a jump, but den a say he must be really change a mean ter say, ter hear him say a ting like dat, an a have ter believe im, after all is a ting i say meself, so a say well he really learn now, he really get de message, well boy tings start ter go good, a get me children in a school, me woman open she laundrette, an de man en even going near me meters, if he want ter go ter de W.C. in de back just not ter pass de meter, de man going through de front door an going round, just not ter pass me meters, da is ter tell yer how good de man get, an he get nice, he get nice ter everybody, he start ter say tank you, ter everybody, an smiling ter everybody, an dat en all he get a job as a nightwatchman in a factory an he even come home an say how nice de foreman is, yer could beat dat, well he beat it, he even get a job fer me modder on de factory bench, so wha a could say ter dat, a could only say well tings like, never say die, an wonders never cease, an wen mango ripe it go fall, anyhow dat en all de man even start ter pay me back me money, not in big pieces but a one here a one dere, but dat was good dat shows he was trying, he heart was in de right place, anyhow i stop tinking bout im, but an wen a say but a mean but yer no, one day de man pay me back a five pound note an wen a look at de five pound note well a had ter look yer no, because he never pay me back so much, wen a look at de five pound note, a see it was de same five pound note a give me wife ter put in de bank fer me, so dat hit me but a figure she must be change some money fer him, so i en worry bout it, but an a say but again yer no, de men start ter pay me back one set a five pound notes, an all a dem is wha a give she ter put in de bank so pardner a ask yer wha a go do, wha you woulda do if all de five pound note you give yer wife ter put in de bank yer see turning up in another man hand, an is a man yer help, i help de man yer no, tell me wha you woulda do, (*Slight pause.*) yer can tink a notten, well i go tell yer wha i do or wha i was going ter do, a was going ter go over ter de pub an buy im a guinness an tell im do kill yer self, but

yer no wat happen, wen a get in de pub, de man in de pub say dey do' serve black people in dis bar i have ter go round, so a hit im, an wen a hit im, he fall against a whole pile a boxes an de whole bar mash up, so da is wat a in dis prison for, well boy a really learn me lesson, da is de last time a go ever be nice anybody.

A bell rings and the man gets up and walks out singing.

I love you baby
I need you baby.

The End.

RUM AN' COCA COLA

Rum an' Coca Cola was first staged at the Royal Court Theatre, London on 3 November 1976, with the following cast:

BIRD	Trevor Thomas
CREATOR	Norman Beaton

Directed by Donald Haworth

The action takes place on a beach in Trinidad.

ACT ONE

Scene One

Beach. Daytime.
Two black men, one about twenty-five, the
other, forty. Rum bottle on the ground.
They are sitting on a fallen coconut
tree.
Guitars on the ground. They are dressed
in bright coloured shirts, straw hats, ragged
trousers.

BIRD (*twenty-five*): Crime does not pay.

CREATOR (*forty*): No, no, no.

BIRD: Ah Man an Woman.

CREATOR: No, a did dat in '65.

BIRD: Give me a drink.

CREATOR (*he passes the bottle*): Here.

BIRD: Politics.

CREATOR: Nah, man, notten now en happening, anybody take bribe lately?

BIRD: No.

CREATOR: Any Minister got catch wid anodder man wife?

BIRD: Yes, Fellows.

CREATOR: Wat he is de Minister of?

BIRD: Works an Communications.

CREATOR: Dat's good, le me see, whey a dey catch dem?

BIRD: At she home she servant catch dem, an she wen an sack de servant for not nocking, an de servant spread de message.

CREATOR: Wha is de servant name?

BIRD: Ruby.

CREATOR: Le me see,

(*Sings:*) A Pretty Lady call Ruby,
Was doing she housework –

A want someting for Ruby.

BIRD: Nicely.

CREATOR:
A Pretty Lady call Ruby
Was doing she housework nicely –

'Nicely', I en sure.

BIRD: Tidily.

CREATOR: Wat is dat?

BIRD: Is a word.

CREATOR: I en no it.

BIRD: Is a word.

CREATOR: You make it up.

BIRD: No, it from tidy, her tidy up, keeps tidy, tidily.

CREATOR: I en like it.

BIRD: Why?

CREATOR: It too high class.

BIRD: Dat en bad, da is point, professors an tings does come ter de tents.

CREATOR: Yer tink so?

BIRD: A no so, Wisdom do use dem kinda words, people go tink you educated.

CREATOR: A no, but dey might tink a too educated.

BIRD: Nar, man.

CREATOR: Okay.

(*Sings:*) A Pretty Lady call Ruby
Was doing she housework tidily –

A still en like it.

BIRD: Awright wat den, clumsily?

CREATOR: Wat is dat?

BIRD: Da is anodder word.

CREATOR: Wa, I go get it,
A Pretty Lady call Ruby
Was doing she housework like a lady.
Yes,
A Pretty Lady call Ruby
Was doing she housework like a lady.

BIRD: Yer say 'lady' aready.

CREATOR: A could say it again.

BIRD: People go say yer can' rhyme, yer run outa words.

CREATOR: Let dem say wat dey want, my record good, my record still stand '65, '66, '67. three in a row, who beat dat, anybody ever beat dat?

BIRD: No, Creator.

CREATOR: So wha yer talking bout, can rhyme, there.

BIRD: Yes, Creator.

CREATOR: Right, we go say 'like a lady'.

BIRD: Yes.

CREATOR (*sings*):
A Pretty Lady call Ruby
Was doing she housework like a lady.

BIRD: Yes.

CREATOR: She – she wat?

BIRD:
She finish clean de pantry –

CREATOR: Yes, yes.

BIRD:
An decided ter do de . . .

CREATOR: No, dat en go work.

BIRD: No, yer right.

CREATOR: Of course a right, I been doing dis long time yer no.

BIRD: Yes, Creator.

CREATOR: Wen you was still running bout in short pants.

BIRD: Yes, Creator.

CREATOR: Give me a drink. 'Decided', wey you get dem big words from, all you youngsters do' no how ter teach people. You have ter use everyday words yer can' use no big word.

BIRD: But Creator, 'decided' en a big word.

CREATOR: I tink a big word, an I should say no.

BIRD: Creator long time 'decided' was a big word, but –

CREATOR: Wha yer mean long time, how old you is?

BIRD: I is twenty-five Creator.

CREATOR: How old you tink I is?

BIRD: I en no Creator, a been hearing bout you for a long time.

CREATOR: Dat do' mean notten, I started young, I in dis business a long time, I is forty, forty en old, forty is prime.

BIRD: Yes, Creator.

CREATOR: Conqueror was still singing wen he was eighty an he was de best.

BIRD: A never hearin, Creator.

CREATOR: You never hear Conqueror?

BIRD: No.

CREATOR: Yer miss someting, dat Man used ter sid down in a room, at two o'clock wid a bottle a rum, an wen dat bottle finish he had ten calypso write down. Dat was a Boss, dat was calypso fadder. You never her im?

BIRD: No.

CREATOR: No wonder you want ter use all dem kinda big words, 'decided', foolish.

A Pretty Lady call Ruby
Was doing she housework, happily.

Yes, a like dat.

BIRD: Yes.

CREATOR: Yer see da is how ter do it, a no a didn't like tidily.

BIRD: Yes, Creator.

CREATOR: Happily better, it innocent yer see, afor telling people she's a good servant, because she happy in she work.

BIRD: Yes, Creator.

CREATOR: So wen de time come, dey go like she.

BIRD: Yes Creator, a see.

CREATOR (*sings*):
A Pretty Lady call Ruby
Was doing she housework happily,
She –

BIRD: What? She Mistress,

She Mistress was making it heavenly.

CREATOR: Making it wha is dat?

BIRD: Da is a new expression.

CREATOR: I never hear it.

BIRD: All de young people does use it.

CREATOR: I en like, it en right.

BIRD: But Creator yer have ter appeal ter young people yer no, is dem who decides wat good nowadays.

CREATOR: Dey decide, for who, not for me, I decide, Creator decides wat good for Creator, dey could decide for odder people but not for me, I decide if someting good, an a sing it if dey en like it, dat do' worry me, I been doin dis for thirty years an always no wat good.

BIRD: Yes, Creator.

CREATOR: So an yer better remember dat if ya going ter get anywhere, is you decide, not young people.

BIRD: Awright Creator.

CREATOR: A like you 'Heavenly'.

BIRD: Yes.

CREATOR: Dat good, she enjoying it.

BIRD: Yes.

CREATOR: It make it nicer wen she get catch.

BIRD: Yes.

CREATOR: But I en like 'making it'.

BIRD: No Creator.

CREATOR: It too hashy, too modern, le me see.

(*Sings*:) A Pretty Lady call Ruby
Was doing she housework happily,
She Mistress was taking it –

'Taking it', dat better,

(*Sings*:) She Mistress was taking it heavenly.

People go no wha yer means.

BIRD: Yes.

CREATOR:
She Mistress was taking it heavenly –

Wat?

BIRD: De Master.

CREATOR: Yes, so people go no wat going on, is bacchanal.

De Master was out –

No, we want –

BIRD:
De Master was working busily.

CREATOR: No dey go tink it was he an she.

BIRD: Yes.

CREATOR:
De Master was out –

BIRD:
– Wit he honey.

CREATOR: Yes, dat could do,

De Master was out wit he honey.

No,

De Master was out making money.

Yer see.

BIRD: Yes.

CREATOR:
De Master was out making money.

Yer see people go feel sorry for him.

BIRD: Yes.

CREATOR: An dey go feel is good he wife get catch.

BIRD: Yes, Creator.

CREATOR: De Man, working hard for he house an family an de bad woman doing ting behind he back.

BIRD: Yes, yes.

CREATOR: So we have.

A Pretty Lady call Ruby
Was doing she housework happily,
She Mistress was taking it heavenly,
She Master was out making money.

I en like 'doing she housework', it out time.

BIRD: Yes.

CREATOR: So we have to leave out 'she'.

A Pretty Lady call Ruby
Was doing housework happily.

You see, now she's servant, yer no dat no.

A Pretty Lady call Ruby
Was doing housework happily,
She Mistress was taking it heavenly,
She Master was out making money.

BIRD: Yes, it coming good.

CREATOR:
Ruby decide –

BIRD: Creator, you en tink 'decide' too big.

CREATOR: Nar, is a good word, 'decided' too big, but not 'decide'.

BIRD: Awright.

CREATOR:
Ruby decide to go inside.

BIRD: Yes, an dis wat she saw.

CREATOR: 'Saw', whey dat come in?

BIRD: Ruby see dem.

CREATOR: Well say dat, say see she see,

Ruby decide to go inside

And dis wat she see.

BIRD: Yes, yes.

CREATOR: See, she see, we have it.

BIRD: Creator look some tourist coming up de beach.

CREATOR: So wat?

BIRD: Le we go.

CREATOR: No man Bird, we have ter finish, let dem focking tourist go way.

BIRD: Le we go Creator, we have to.

CREATOR: You go, I go stay here an –

BIRD: No Creator, two a we have ter, is better wid two playing an yer no, dey go give more if two a we go, dan one.

CREATOR: Awright, wat?

BIRD: 'Rum an Coca Cola'.

CREATOR *and* BIRD *stand. We do not see the tourists.* CREATOR *and* BIRD *sing 'Rum an Coca Cola', and 'Mary Ann.'*

BIRD: Tank you Marm, tanks Joe, hope you enjoy your stay.

CREATOR *and* BIRD *back off and return to their seats.*

CREATOR: How much we get?

BIRD: A dollar.

CREATOR: U.S.?

BIRD: No, Trinidad.

CREATOR: Focking Americans day smart yer no, dey change all dey money soon dey land. (*Imitating:*) 'We must get some local currency, where can we change some Travellers Cheques, look at she big bottom, a do' no how she get in dem pants, she must have bout four girdle.' Dem Yankee women like ter fock yer no.

BIRD: Yes.

CREATOR: An dey does give yer a tip, I used ter sing in a hotel, an dey does come up an ask fer request always wait ter hear 'Mary Ann'. 'Mary Ann', as though dey had no odder calypso but 'Mary Ann' and 'Rum an Coca Cola'. Once one a dem give a waiter a message ter give me, if I would come ter she room, an play for she after de show.

BIRD: You went?

CREATOR: I went. In dem days, yer went behind any ting, especially American.

BIRD: An wha happens?

CREATOR: I play fer she, wen a went in she was wearing a night gown.

BIRD: No.

CREATOR: Yes.

BIRD: You fock she?

CREATOR: Yes I fock all a dem, da was part a de job, all a dem who wanted yer had ter do it.

BIRD: An wha happen, dey pay you?

CREATOR: Some a dem, dey would say tanks an give yer dollar, some a dem used ter take yer address an say dey go send for you, dat you could get job singing in Night Club in de States.

BIRD: An wha happen?

CREATOR: None a dem never write, it never happen. Focking Yankee, dey smart, but I had a good time.

BIRD: Creator, you had a real interesting life, real experience.

CREATOR: Yes plenty ting happen ter me. Go an buy anodder bottle den le we try an finish dis calypso.

BIRD: Awright.

BIRD *goes.* CREATOR *sings.*

CREATOR:
A Pretty Lady call Ruby
Was doing housework happily,
She Mistress was taking it heavenly,
She Master was out making money,
Ruby decide to go inside,
An dis is wat she see –
An dis is wat she see.

Wat keeping dat boy he so slow, a do' no why a bodder try teach im, an dis is wat she see. A send for a rum he take two years an dis is wat she see, keeping im, she see, she see . . .

BIRD *returns with a bottle.*

Wat keep you so long?

BIRD: Creator a tink a pick up –

CREATOR: Pick up wat, wat you going picking up, I send you fer a bottle you pick up.

BIRD: A was —

CREATOR: Do' forget we have a calypso ter finish.

BIRD: No, no, but a meet –

CREATOR: In de bottle break de seal now.

BIRD: Awright Creator.

BIRD *opens the bottle, drinks from it and passes it to* CREATOR.

CREATOR: Now we reach: an dis is wat she see.

BIRD: Yes, de Minister –

CREATOR: A wat?

BIRD: Works an Communications.

CREATOR: Right.

An dis is wat she see,
De Minister a Works an Communications –

Nar dat too long.

BIRD: Yes.

CREATOR: We have ter break it up.

BIRD: Wha bout

An dis wat she see:
It was –

CREATOR: Yes, it was –

De Minister Works an Communications

BIRD: Yes.

CREATOR: He works was working –

BIRD: Yes.

CREATOR: An he Communicator was Communicating

BIRD: Yes.

CREATOR: An wat?

BIRD: An de Mistress –

CREATOR: Yes, le we see –

Ruby decide to go inside
An dis is wat she see:
It was de Minister a Works an Communications,
He Works was Working,
He Communicator was Communicating
An de Mistress –

BIRD:
– Was shaking.

CREATOR: Yes, good, good, we no wat going on,

De Mistress was shaking –

Le we see

Ruby decides to go inside
An dis is wat she see:
De Minister –

BIRD: No,

It was –

CREATOR: Right.

It was de Minister a Works an Communications
He Works was Working
He Communicator was Communicating
An de Mistress was shaking.

BIRD: Ruby –

CREATOR: Yes.

BIRD: Ruby, Ruby forget to nock –

CREATOR: Nar, a do' like it.

BIRD: Why?

CREATOR: A like nock,

Ruby didn't nock
De Minister pull out he –

BIRD: We can' say dat.

CREATOR: A no, a no.

BIRD: We go get lock up.

CREATOR: Yes, you no long time we coulda say it, in de old day.

BIRD: We could say chicken.

CREATOR:
Ruby did'nt nock,
De Minister pull out he chicken –

Yes we have ter say chicken.

BIRD: Wat used ter happen long time wen you say dem words?

CREATOR: Notten, people used ter laugh everybody no calypso was dirty, everybody like dirty calypso, is only nowadays yer can' say certain tings, long time it use ter be who could be dirtiest.

BIRD: Yes.

CREATOR: People used ter bawl an scream wen yer hit dem a dirty word, I see women wet de self, wen Calypsonian singing already.

BIRD: Creator give me a drink.

CREATOR (*passes the bottle*): Yes Man.

BIRD *passes the bottle.*

I sing Government House once.

CREATOR *drinks.*

BIRD: You sing Government House?

CREATOR: Yes.

BIRD: You sing calypso in Government House?

CREATOR: Yes.

BIRD: I didn't no dat.

CREATOR: Yes, de Governor ask for a Cabaret, dey have steel band, an two Calypsonian, me an roving minstrel, I en talking bout yesterday yer no, I talking bout 1950 – wen calypso start getting respectable, is de Governor who do it, he ask for calypso.

BIRD: I didn't no dat.

CREATOR: Yes, an all dem white Trinidadians, dey copy, dey mimic, wen dey see de Governor like calypso all a dem start ter like it, an start coming ter de tent, but before dat it only black people like calypso, now you go in de tent is only white people yer see black people can' afford ter go in de tent no more.

BIRD: Da is true.

CREATOR: Ah tell you someting else, I had two tunes dat year one a dem was a kinda naughty story bout a boy an a girl, an de odder one was rude, it was bout a preacher wife an she Alsatian dog.

BIRD: I en no dat one.

CREATOR: Is a old one, an de white Portuguese man who de Governor ask ter get, say a musn't sing dat one, a musn't embarrass no-one an notten smutty at Government House must go on.

BIRD: Yes.

CREATOR: Trinidadian foolish yer no, dey always want ter pretend dey is somebody good somebody who do' do notting.

BIRD: Yes, wha happen?

CREATOR: I sing me first tune, an de governor come over ter me an say he hope a go sing de Alsatian tune.

BIRD: *No.*

CREATOR: Yes.

BIRD: How he hear it?

CREATOR: Da is wat a ask im, he hear one a de servants singing it an he ask she de words, an da was favourite calypso.

BIRD: An you sings it?

CREATOR: Yes, a never sing so sweet, in ma life.

BIRD: Dat great man.

CREATOR: An you no de first man ter start clapping an jumping was de Trinidad man Portuguese.

BIRD: Yes?

CREATOR: He say da was de best calypso he ever hear, an how he proud a me, a didn't let him down.

BIRD: Yes, calypso in Government House.

CREATOR: Yes, an a police car drive me home too, yes.

BIRD: Creator you really live man, I en no notten bout dem days.

CREATOR: Dey was good good days, dem days, calypsonian was like a hero, everybody like you, everybody no, nowadays it all records an television an radio, people do' no dem.

BIRD: Times change Creator, yer have ter move wid de times.

CREATOR: Not me, I en moving, le we finish we calypso.

BIRD: Awright.

CREATOR: Yer no if it come out good you could enter it for competition.

BIRD: Who go sing it?

CREATOR: You.

BIRD: Me?

CREATOR: Yes you, an you want to be a Calypsonian de best way is ter win a competition.

BIRD: But Creator –

CREATOR: You fraid?

BIRD: No, but I en feel a ready.

CREATOR: I go no if you ready, if I say you ready you ready, a say if it turn out good.

BIRD: Awright, why do' you sing it Creator?

CREATOR: Me, not me, my days done, I can' keep up wid dem youngsters a could sing wid, a could compose better dan dem, but ter win competition nowadays yer have wear all kinda tight pants wit lurex shirts and frills an sequins all over you like a Christmas tree. I can' do dat.

BIRD: But da is part a de show, Creator.

CREATOR: Not for me, I is Calypsonian, not show off.

BIRD: Is wat people like Creator.

CREATOR: Not me, pass da bottle, dem kill calypso.

BIRD *passes the bottle.*

BIRD: Some more tourist coming Creator.

CREATOR: We have a half-bottle let dem pass, Bird.

BIRD: No Creator we have ter go.

CREATOR: You like too much money boy.

BIRD: We have ter live Creator an is good experience for me.

CREATOR: I giving you good experience.

BIRD: Yes Creator, but we could buy anodder bottle.

CREATOR: Awright le we go, wha we doing?

They get up.

BIRD: 'Mary Ann', 'Coca Cola'.

CREATOR *and* BIRD *stand, sing.*

BIRD: Tank you Joe, tank you Joe, enjoy your stay.

They back in, bowing, they sit.

CREATOR: Focking Yankee.

BIRD: Yankee en bad, at least dey does give we money.

CREATOR: How much you get?

BIRD: A dollar.

CREATOR: Da is anodder bottle.

BIRD: You ever sing for English people Creator?

CREATOR: I sing for everybody, Italian, Spanish, German, everybody, all a dem give me money.

BIRD: Wha bout de English?

CREATOR: English do' give money, dey say tank you, an shake you hand.

BIRD: Yes, dey poor like we.

CREATOR: Dey en poor dey tight. Whey we reach?

BIRD: I can' remember.

CREATOR: You have ter remember, you no your brains young, you have ter remember.

BIRD:
De Minister pull out he chicken –

CREATOR: Yes, yes.

Ruby didn't nock
De Minister pull out he chicken –

BIRD: Yes, Yes.

CREATOR: We have ter pause at chicken, give dem some suspense.

BIRD: Yes.

CREATOR:
De Minister pull out he chicken.
   Wat –

BIRD:
De Mistress –

CREATOR: Wat? Chicken, da is hard one.

BIRD: Yes, de Mistress was feeling –

CREATOR: Nar,
De Mistress say you cheating.

BIRD: Cheating – Chicken – dat en sound right.

CREATOR: Wat den?

BIRD:
De Minister pull out he chicken,
De Mistress say you cheating –

CREATOR: Yes man.

BIRD: Ruby –

CREATOR:
So she give Ruby de sack.

BIRD: Yes Creator we have it. Number One, you could really write calypso.

CREATOR: Yes de old still have some tunes in he head, you go have ter sing it do'.

BIRD: Awright.

He drinks.

CREATOR: You could remember it.

BIRD: Yes.

CREATOR: Awright, stand up an le me see you sing it.

BIRD (*gets up*):
A Pretty Lady call Ruby
Was doing housework happily,
She Mistress was taking it heavenly,
She Master was out making money,
Ruby decide to go inside,
An dis is wat she see:
It was de Minister a Works an Communications,
He works was working,
He Communicator was Communicating,
An de Mistress was shaking,
Ruby didn't nock,
De Minister pull out he – chicken,
De Mistress say you cheating,
So she give Ruby de sack.

CREATOR: Yes, yes, it good.

BIRD: How a do Creator?

CREATOR: You do good but you must use you hand more, ter punch de words.

BIRD: Like dis? (*He points his finger.*)

CREATOR: Yes.

BIRD: Creator a really like it you no, I en feel scared at all, a could do it, I en nervous.

CREATOR: Yes well singing in front a me is notten, but singing in front a ten thousand people, wid bright lights, an a big band is anodder ting.

BIRD: A could do it Creator, a could do it.

CREATOR: We go see.

BIRD: How you do it Creator, how you stan in front a all dem people an sing?

CREATOR: I no I was good, a was nervous, but a no my tune was good, you bound to be nervous, but wen dey call yer name, an de crowd roar, an de band start ter play, pardner you en have time ter be nervous, you have ter sing, an da is it, you could shit yerself, wen you finish, but yer have ter sing.

BIRD: How yer feel wen you win Creator, wen you no for sure wen day say it, how you feel?

CREATOR: De first time, da was it, da was de best. I win three time you no, but de first time, a king, a feel like a king, wen dey put de crown on you head, an de cape round you shoulders, an de band start ter play you tune an you have ter sing it again, but dis time, you win, da is how it feel.

BIRD: Yes.

CREATOR: Da is how it feel.

BIRD: Three times.

CREATOR: An fer dat whole year, everybody no you, everybody talk ter you, wen you walk down de street people call wha happening Creator, how you is, Creator, you see king.

BIRD: Yes?

CREATOR: If you go in a rum shop, is 'Wha you drinking?' 'Le me buy you a drink'. People queuing up ter buy you drink, da is wat it like.

BIRD: Yes, a see.

CREATOR: You see, you tink you could do dat Bird?

BIRD: Yes, Creator, I could do it, a no.

CREATOR: Awright let me get a sleep, we a wake up, we go see.

BIRD: Yes, Creator.

CREATOR *nods off.*

Scene Two

The beach later. Evening.
CREATOR *is still asleep.*
BIRD *returns carrying a paper bag.*

BIRD: Creator, Creator wake up, wake up. (*Shaking him.*)

CREATOR: Wha happening, wha happening? Wha is it?

BIRD: Is me, Bird.

CREATOR (*getting up*): Wha happen, Bird?

BIRD: Is time ter get up.

CREATOR: Why?

BIRD: A bring you someting ter eat man.

CREATOR: Yes, yes, wha is it?

BIRD: Is some roti.

CREATOR: Yes.

BIRD *gives* CREATOR *rotis.*

CREATOR: De rum finish?

BIRD: No, an a bring anodder bottle for later.

CREATOR: Good. Ahh. (*Stretches.*) A was having a nice dream man.

BIRD: I had a nice time too.

CREATOR: Wha you went?

BIRD: A went in de village.

CREATOR: You see anybody.

BIRD: Yes, a few tourist was in de bar. Mano wanted ter no if we coming.

CREATOR: Wha you tell im?

BIRD: A tell im soon.

CREATOR: Why you tell im dat, I en feel like going tonight, wha is de time?

BIRD: Bout nine.

CREATOR: Yes, a had a good sleep. Wha you do?

BIRD: A had a swim en wat.

CREATOR: In de sea?

BIRD: Yes.

CREATOR: Why you do dat?

BIRD: A needed it, an den a went for a walk. A went down ter Golden Arrow, de place look full Creator.

CREATOR: Full a wat?

BIRD: Tourist Creator.

CREATOR: How you no dey is tourist, dey could be night people.

BIRD: No, a went up by de side a de dance floor, an dey is tourist, so dat mean tomorrow we go be busy.

CREATOR: Maybe, we have a calypso ter finish you no.

BIRD: I no.

CREATOR: So we should rest.

BIRD: No, man, we have plenty time, why you en go an have a swim Creator, you might feel better.

CREATOR: Wha me swim? Never, me, en going in dat sea.

BIRD: It might wake you up.

CREATOR: Who want to wake up? Whey de rum?

BIRD: Here. Creator you no dey say if you bathe in de sea, after dark, is does wash way you bad luck.

CREATOR: Who say?

BIRD: People, people say.

CREATOR: Not me, I want my bad luck, a keeping my bad luck, you en catching me in dat sea.

BIRD: Creator we going soon.

CREATOR: Where.

BIRD: To Mano bar.

CREATOR: A taught we wasn't going ternight.

BIRD: We have ter go, is work.

CREATOR: Why you so worry, Mano do' pay no money.

BIRD: It en dat man, is de experience a need an you remember dis morning a tell you a pick up.

CREATOR: No.

BIRD: Well a tell you, you must be forget. Well a was talking ter dis girl, she was asking me bout we tunes an tings wey de come from if dey handed down an ting, an whey me learn to play guitar.

CREATOR: So wat?

BIRD: Well she at Mano wid she modder and fadder.

CREATOR: So wat?

BIRD: So a want ter go an sing you see, a want she ter see me sing, in a club.

CREATOR: Bird a tell dem ting do lead ter notten.

BIRD: A no but is experience.

CREATOR: Awright we go go.

BIRD: Tanks Creator.

CREATOR: Do' tank me is work. Whey she from?

BIRD: New Jersey.

CREATOR: Well le we go den, if we is professional Calypsonians singing for money, le we go.

They get up, going off.

BIRD: Wha you dream, Creator?

CREATOR: A go tell you anodder time.

They go off.

ACT TWO

Scene One

Mano's Bar. A stage. We do not see the audience. CREATOR *and* BIRD *are on stage.*

BIRD: Tank you ladies and gentlemen, is nice ter see so many happy smiling faces at Mano's ternight, if is calypso you want you come ter de right place, if is any ting you want Mano is de place ter come but ternight is calypso, is calypso you want is calypso you go get. A have here wit me, an is honour, one a de greatest Calypsonian Trinidad ever produced, if not de greatest, de mighty Creator, a big hand everybody (BIRD *starts clapping.* CREATOR *steps forward, doffs hat, steps back.*) for de mighty Creator, de mighty Creator, we go now play some a everybody's favourite.

They sing 'Rum an Coca Cola' and 'Mary Ann', one verse, one chorus.

BIRD: Tank you very much ladies an gentlemen, a said it was a great honour ter have de mighty Creator an a mean it, as you go see, I will now hand you over ter de mighty Creator, who will give you a idea a wat real calypso is like an why he win King Calypso three times running, ladies an gentlemen a big hand, de mighty Creator.

BIRD *starts to go off.* CREATOR *holds him back.*

CREATOR: Whey you going?

BIRD: A going ter have a drink.

CREATOR: Do' take long.

BIRD *goes.*

CREATOR *steps forward.*

CREATOR: Tank you ladies an gentlemen, a lota people an dem, say calypso dying out dat de young generation do' want calypso no more, but I say as long as we have young Calypsonian like Bird, calypso go live forever. Bird say I win three times running an he en lie, an a would like ter sing de calypso dat stop it from being four times running, de one dat beat me a lot a dem odder Calypsonian jealous, dey do sing older people tune, but I en jealous, Creator en jealous, a nobody except Creator an Creator go sing it ter show you wat kinda competition he was up against, ladies an gentlemen, 'Jonah an de Bake' by de mighty Spoiler.

For de tourist in de audience Creator would just like ter say a bake is a small ting make outa flour, like a pancake, but it salt it en sweet. 'Jonah an de Bake.'

CREATOR *sings 'Jonah an de Bake' by Spoiler. He finishes.* BIRD *jumps on to the stage.*

BIRD: Tank you ladies en gentlemen, Mano's will now treat you ter some a his great records an we will take a break, dose dat feel like dancing de floor is yours, tank you.

CREATOR *sits on the stage.* BIRD *sits.*

CREATOR: Wha happen, whey de girl, why you en dancing?

BIRD: She sitting over dey.

CREATOR: Why you en dancing?

BIRD: Mano.

CREATOR: Wha happen ter him?

BIRD: He say he en want no Calypsonian dancing wid he customer.

CREATOR: Dat modder ass, a go fix him, a tell you we shouldn't a come.

BIRD: Is awright, a make a date.

CREATOR: For wen?

BIRD: Later.

CREATOR: Good. She have money?

BIRD: It look so, she buy me a drink, a look inside she purse.

CREATOR: Dat en notting, tourist always have money on dem, wha she clothes like, wha she shoes like, what she jewellery like, dem is de kinda tings you must look for.

BIRD: She looks nice, she look expensive, en she wearing gold, she have a gold chain an a gold watch.

CREATOR: Dat sound good, whey you meeting she?

BIRD: By de lagoon.

CREATOR: Well you go an keep you date, I go finish here an go home.

BIRD: She want ter meet you, a promise.

CREATOR: A do' want ter meet she.

BIRD: But Creator, a promise.

CREATOR: Who tell you promise, a say a do' want ter meet she, an do' bring she home, now go an keep you date.

BIRD: Awright, Creator.

BIRD *goes.* CREATOR *staggers on stage.*

CREATOR: Ladies an gentlemen I de mighty Creator will now sing some tunes for you, not for Mano dat tief an crook but for you, an if Creator say he going en do someting he does do it, dey was a time you no, wen Creator was de greatest Calypsoman in de world, an wen Mano offer him a hundred dollars a week ter sing in he Club, but Creator say no, he was singing in a better Club, wid nicer tables wid candles on dem, an waiters coming ter you table, an you had ter wear a tie, Mano can run no bar, because he is a crook an a tief, he feel he is somebody but he en nobody, Mano – I no Mano, wen he . . .

Scene Two

The beach later.
CREATOR *is sleeping.*
BIRD *returns.*

BIRD: Creator, Creator you sleeping.

CREATOR *murmurs.*

Wake up now Man, you en want ter hear how a do?

CREATOR: Wat? Wat? Who?

BIRD: Is me, Bird.

CREATOR: Yes, yes. Wat you want?

BIRD: A want ter tell you how a make out.

CREATOR: Tell me in de morning. A –

BIRD: You awright?

CREATOR: Yes I awright. If you want ter tell me, tell me now, a go listen.

BIRD: A meet she, she keep de date.

CREATOR *murmurs.*

An de first ting a went for was a quick kill.

CREATOR *murmurs.*

But she say, no, she want ter talk first, an we have a lot a time for dat. Creator dat ever happen ter you?

CREATOR *murmurs.*

Well anyhow we talk, an she tell me how she life is in New Jersey, she live in New Jersey, but she work in New York, you see, an I tell she wat my life is like here in Trinidad an she say I lucky. Creator you listening?

CREATOR *murmurs.*

Creator.

CREATOR: Yes, yes.

BIRD: Yes, she say we lucky, but it can' last, dat life en like dat, times change, she's twenty-five, you no dat, so young an de girl have plenty ideas.

CREATOR *murmurs.*

She's a secretary an she here for anodder week.

CREATOR: You fock she?

BIRD: No.

CREATOR: Why?

BIRD: She say she do' like one night stands, an if da is all I want, she would do it but a won't see she again, is up ter me.

CREATOR: You shoulda fock she man.

BIRD: No, Creator, dis girl really like me, dis girl really sensible, she en no tourist.

CREATOR: Wha she doing here den?

BIRD: She on holiday, she tell me, an dis is between me an you you here.

CREATOR: Wat?

BIRD: She was ter get married ter a boy an call it off, so she modder an fadder bring she on holiday, so you see she en no tourist.

CREATOR (*murmurs*): All a dem is tourist.

BIRD: Wat?

CREATOR: All a dem is tourist.

BIRD: But Creator, you en hear nothing yet. You no wat?

CREATOR: Wat, she want ter take you back wid she?

BIRD: No, not right away, I no want you tinking but dis girl en like dem old Jock en Jem dat you used ter meet up wid.

CREATOR: Wat she is?

BIRD (*lies down*): Me en telling you

nothing, you tink because one ting happen ter you de same ting go happen ter me, you en no dis girl.

A beat.

By de way, wha was all de fuss about down at Mano's? A pass dey an a see all table's out-side break up.

CREATOR: It wasn't no fuss, Mano an me had a row, an he put he boys on me.

BIRD: Wha was de row about? You awright?

CREATOR: I awright, let me go ter sleep.

BIRD: You sure?

CREATOR: Yes.

A beat.

BIRD: A teaching she how ter swim termorrow.

CREATOR *snores.*

Scene Three

Morning, the beach.
BIRD *wakes up, looks at* CREATOR. *There is blood on his face, and shirt.*

BIRD: Oh shit Creator, Creator, wake up. (*He shakes him.*) Wake up.

CREATOR: What happening?

BIRD: Is morning man, an you face. Mano an the boys really beat you man, oh shit yes shit. Get up Creator, get up man.

CREATOR (*getting up*): A tell you we had a row.

BIRD: Oh shit, man, get up, you face. No, do' move, a get some water.

BIRD *takes an empty rum bottle, goes to the sea, returns, pours water on* CREATOR's *face.*

Oh shit man, wha you do, you face all beat up, you eye, oh shit.

CREATOR: I awright, a tell you.

BIRD: You en awright.

BIRD *tears his shirt, cleans his face, using the water.*

You is a mess.

CREATOR: Wha is dat?

BIRD: Is sea water, watch it sting.

CREATOR: Yes.

BIRD: Dat mean it working, oh shit man wha happen?

CREATOR: Notten happen.

BIRD: Wha you mean, notten happen? Mano beat you up for notten?

CREATOR: A tell you we had a row.

BIRD (*moves*): A going down a see Mano.

CREATOR: No, do' go.

BIRD: Well tell me.

CREATOR: A tell im I en like de way he treat you.

BIRD: Treat me?

CREATOR: Yes, a tell im he shoulda let you sit down en dance wid de girl.

BIRD: But Creator, I didn't mind.

CREATOR: But I mind.

BIRD: Oh shit Creator.

CREATOR: You is my boy, a training you, you wid me, an if a take you somewhere people should treat you wid respect, if dey want me in dey place dey must do dat.

BIRD: Shut you mouth Creator.

CREATOR: So a tell im, he say I can' tell im how ter run he bar.

BIRD: So alyer had a fight?

CREATOR: Yes.

BIRD: An he boys join in an dey throw you out?

CREATOR: Yes.

BIRD: Creator, you is a real ass, a didn't mind wha Mano do, it suit me, it mean a had ter meet she outside by she self, it suit me, now we lose de only steady work we had.

CREATOR: Dat en true man, Mano would always take me back, because I is de best Calypsoman by reputation.

BIRD: No, Creator, oh shit, well a clean you face de best a could, go in de sea an wash off.

CREATOR: Nar, I en going in de sea, I go be awright.

BIRD: Da is up ter you.

They sit staring out to sea.
A beat.

BIRD: Creator wha we go do?

CREATOR: How you mean?

BIRD: Mano, Mano a mean, how we go eat? We en go get enough on de beach.

CREATOR: We go make it, do' worry.

BIRD: Dat was sure work, dat was certain work.

CREATOR: Do' worry man, Bird, we go make it, do' mind Mano, he en nobody, he go come crawling back ter we begging we ter play, an you girl say we good.

BIRD: She saw we good but you en no Mano, he hard.

CREATOR: Do' worry we go survive, an you say you see plenty tourist, we go make it.

BIRD: But Creator I can' do it alone, an you can' do it. Look at you, you have blood all over you, you can' go in front tourist.

CREATOR: You could do it, if you wanted ter.

BIRD: No, man.

CREATOR: A tell you, a didn't want ter tell you before, because you might get big-headed, but you good you know.

BIRD: Creator.

CREATOR: No, a mean it, you good. A ever lie ter you?

BIRD: No.

CREATOR: Yes, you good, you no how ter hold a crowd, you have a nice smile, an you have a good voice, an is dem tings count.

BIRD: No, Creator.

CREATOR: Look do' tell me, no, I no, I singing calypso longer dan you, I no wat count, you remind me a me wen I was just starting, de same style. Why you feel I take you on. You feel I en no notting?

BIRD: No, Creator, you no a lot, I tink you no more bout calypso dan anybody else in Trinidad, but I no, I can' take on a crowd by meself, I no dat.

CREATOR: You scared.

BIRD: No, I en scared, maybe, a might be, but dat en it, I en ready, a could hold me own wid you dey, but not by myself.

CREATOR: A boy, you really let me down. I taught you was a real champion, so I is you fadder, I groom you, I no wen you ready.

BIRD: No, Creator.

CREATOR: Awright, wha you go do?

BIRD: A tink a might go back into town, an see me modder.

CREATOR: You mean, you going back down Frederick Street, an pick pocket.

BIRD: No, wha you go do?

CREATOR: I go be awright, I go do wha a always do, sing calypso. If people want ter give me money da is awright, but I go sing calypso.

BIRD: Awright.

CREATOR: Wha bout de girl?

BIRD: A going an see she now, an tell she. A see you. (*Walks off.*)

CREATOR (*calls out*): You coulda be de best, better dan me, Number One, I coulda make you dat, yer no.

BIRD *goes off.* CREATOR *sits down, takes a drink.*

CREATOR (*to himself*): Focking chicken.

ACT THREE

Scene One

Later, evening. The beach.
CREATOR *is standing singing.*

CREATOR:
A – Pretty Lady – call Ruby
was doing some housework – peace –

BIRD *comes up.*

BIRD: Happily.

CREATOR (*turns*): Happily. Wat you want?

BIRD: Notting.

CREATOR:
– Was doing she homework, happily.

He turns.

Wat you come back for?

BIRD: Notten, an it en homework, is housework

CREATOR: A taught you went back ter town ter pick pocket.

BIRD: A change me mind.

CREATOR: Well a en change mine, I en want you back, I en need you I make ten dollars ter day, all de tourist give me money, ten dollars more dan we ever get tergether, so I en want you back, you could beg me all you want.

BIRD: A should pick you pocket.

CREATOR: Wat you want?

BIRD: A come back ter finish de calypso.

CREATOR: Wat?

BIRD: A come back ter finish Ruby.

CREATOR: Ruby dead.

BIRD: No, we could do it, Creator, we could finish it, an I go sing it fer competition.

CREATOR: Who say so?

BIRD: You.

CREATOR: Wen?

BIRD: Dis morning.

CREATOR: I say so?

BIRD: Yes.

CREATOR: A must a been drunk.

BIRD: No, Creator, you say a could do it.

CREATOR: But how we go live, I en get no tourist.

BIRD: I no, we go get help.

CREATOR: From whey?

BIRD: I go hustle tourist.

CREATOR: By yourself?

BIRD: Yes, an we go get help from Marian, de girl.

CREATOR: Wat girl?

BIRD: De American.

CREATOR: Wat she have ter do wid dis?

BIRD: A fock she.

CREATOR: You shoulda do dat, a long time – da is all?

BIRD: Creator you do' understand, a went an tell she why a was leaving.

CREATOR *sways*.

Look sid down, le me tell you.

CREATOR: No, a can' understand wha she have ter do wid it.

BIRD: She offer, she offer ter help we, look a tell she why a was leaving right, an she say she would help, da is wha you say tourist does do.

CREATOR: Yes, but da is wat dey does say, all.

BIRD: But she mean it, she give me money, look, you see U.S. dollars.

CREATOR: A see, why you fock she?

BIRD: Creator, look, dis money mean we could finish we tune in peace, buy some clothes – a no you en tink we need dem, but you wrong, she agree, an we enter dis year.

CREATOR: An she go stay?

BIRD: No, Creator, she going back, but she go come down for de Competition, an den we go back up.

CREATOR: You an she?

BIRD: Yes Creator, but you go get de fame, because it go be one a your tunes dat win.

CREATOR: How you no it go win?

BIRD: It must, an people go no you still in business.

CREATOR: I en no, I en no. Look some tourist coming, go an hustle dem, le me watch you.

BIRD: I en need ter Creator, we have money.

CREATOR: Yes, yes.

BIRD: Creator, a teach she how ter swim, by de lagoon da is we favourite spot an we lie down by de side an de next ting a no we was naked, no swimsuit, just me an she, you shoulda see me man.

CREATOR: Yes.

BIRD: Creator she hold me like she would'n let go, she waiting dey fer me now, we going an spend de whole night together under de sky. I just come ter give you de news, an see if you awright.

CREATOR: I awright, de rum finish da is all, a just need a drink, before you go go an buy me a bottle wen, I can' go in Mano's.

BIRD: Yes, awright, sure, da is all you want? You en want notten ter eat, a roti?

CREATOR: Nar, nar, just a bottle.

BIRD: Awright.

BIRD *goes*. CREATOR *gets up, goes in the opposite direction.*
BIRD *returns with a bottle.*

BIRD (*calls*): Creator, Creator, where you? Come now man where you? Come now man.

BIRD *sits down*. CREATOR *returns*.

BIRD: Dere you is. Whey you went?

CREATOR: I was in de sea. A went ter wash off.

BIRD: Awright look you rum, a see you later, maybe termorrow.

BIRD *goes off laughing, whistling.* CREATOR *sits down, drinks*. BIRD *returns crying.*

BIRD: She dead Creator.

CREATOR: Bird, what happen?

BIRD: She dead Creator, de girl dead. Marian, Marian dead.

CREATOR: How she dead? How you mean she dead?

BIRD: She dead, she dead. A went up by de

lagoon an a big crowd a people, stand round an police dey, an she dead, she lying down in de sand dead, somebody strangle she.

CREATOR: Who? Who do dat?

BIRD: She dead Creator, all she necklace an watch an ring gone, dey say somebody must be strangle she fer dem.

CREATOR: Oh shit Bird, a sorry, but she was only tourist.

BIRD: She wasn't no focking tourist man, she was a good girl, a girl who was going ter help we, now she dead, Creator life hard.

CREATOR: Bird, listen ter me, do' take so hard man, we could still do it, we could still make it, no matter wha happen, we go still hustle. Dey can' take dat away from we. We could hustle em wen de time come, we could finish me tune an enter it. Ruby en dead, Ruby still alive, we could make she live.

BIRD: No, Creator, we can' do it, not me, I have ter go into town, I have ter go home.

CREATOR: Why Bird?

BIRD: Dey go tink I do it, people must be see we tergether, dey go start ter look –

CREATOR: But you en do it.

BIRD: Of course I en do it, but who go believe dat? You no how people does talk soon as dey see a black man wid a tourist, somebody must say I do it.

CREATOR: I no you en do it, I go tell dem, you was wit me all night, we en move, we sit down here en drink rum, an we en move, so you clear.

BIRD: Tanks Creator but no. A can' stay, it go be too much.

BIRD: But Bird –

CREATOR *grabs* BIRD. BIRD *pushes his hand on* CREATOR's *pocket.*

BIRD: Wha is dat in you pocket?

CREATOR: Is –

BIRD *takes out a gold chain, a gold watch and a gold ring.*

BIRD: Da is Marian gold chain, an gold watch, Creator, an she ring.

CREATOR: Bird listen –

BIRD: Whey you get dem Creator?

CREATOR: Bird –

BIRD: Wha you do Creator? Wha you do? Oh God.

CREATOR: Bird, she was a tour –

BIRD: Why Creator, why? She was going ter help we, she was going ter help we.

CREATOR: She wasn't going ter help me, Bird.

BIRD: Yes, Creator, she was, she was.

CREATOR: Bird –

BIRD: Why Creator, why a want ter no why?

CREATOR: She couldn't help me Bird. Nobody could help me Bird.

BIRD: Why Creator?

CREATOR: Spoiler, Bird. Spoiler do it.

BIRD: Wha you mean?

CREATOR: We couldn't win, not wid Ruby, wen a sing Spoiler tune a no we couldn't win wid Ruby, we couldn't win Bird.

BIRD: Oh shit, Creator.

CREATOR: Is true Bird, a can' write no more tune, de young boys better, it do' matter wat dey wear dey better. We couldn't win.

BIRD: But it didn't matter if we win, is de experience I wanted Creator.

CREATOR: Not me Bird, we had ter win.

BIRD: Oh shit, Creator.

CREATOR *goes towards the sea.*

Whey you going Creator?

CREATOR: A just going ter wash off. A en going far.

BIRD: But Creator –

CREATOR: Do' worry Bird, you go get anodder tourist, de world full a tourist, an all a dem rich.

BIRD: Creator.

CREATOR: Bird, tell dem I do it, you was at Mano's.

BIRD: Creator.

CREATOR: You remember a tell you a had a dream?

BIRD: Creator.

CREATOR: Well a dream, Ruby had ter win, but dat was just a dream. Ruby dead Bird. Ruby dead Bird. Ruby dead. If Creator say so is so.

WELCOME HOME JACKO

Welcome Home Jacko was first staged on 12 June 1979 at The Factory, Paddington, London and subsequently at the Riverside Studios, Hammersmith with the following cast:

JACKO	Gordon Case
MARCUS	Victor Evans
ZIPPY	Trevor Laird
FRET	Alrick Riley
SANDY	Maggie Shevlin
GAIL	Dorrett Thompson
DOLE	Chris Tummings

Directed by Charlie Hanson

Act One

Scene: a Youth Club.
Time: afternoon.
A bar counter on the side with stools, also
tables and chairs against the wall. Posters of
Africa, Ethiopia, Haile Selassie, Youth
Employment, a Police P.R. poster. Across
the ceiling a larger banner saying:
WELCOME HOME JACKO. *The rear*
stairs leading to an office upstairs. In the
corner a Juke Box-Football machine.
Four black boys (seventeen to twenty-one),
ZIPPY, MARCUS, DOLE *and* FRET *are*
playing a football machine.

ZIPPY: Ras Clart me a beat yer.

MARCUS: Bet wat you a miss ter Ras clart, you a hit one ball you a call dat beat.

ZIPPY: Aright, make we play one more game, Dole yer ready?

DOLE: Me no want te play no mor Man, him a make ter much Ras Clart noise make we play some Dominoes.

ZIPPY: Cha Man, I we play.

MARCUS: Me an Fret go clart yer ras, eh Fret?

FRET: Yea, yea, make we play, en last round, first five win.

MARCUS: Wha yer say?

ZIPPY: Me ready Dole.

DOLE: Aright, make we play, him a make ter much noise make we shut him Ras Clart mouth.

MARCUS: Wait, wait, wha we a play for?

ZIPPY: Wha him mean?

MARCUS: Coke, make we play fer Coke, who a lose him have ter buy, wha yer a say?

ZIPPY: Cha why not you no win.

DOLE: Yea.

MARCUS: Make we see.

ZIPPY: Aright.

They play. ZIPPY *and* DOLE, MARCUS *and* FRET.

ZIPPY: Move dey, yer Ras shift, eh.

DOLE: Block him Ras.

MARCUS: Go way Block yer Bomba, dat . . . go in, go in.

ZIPPY: Block him Cha.

MARCUS: Move Fret, block im Fret.

ZIPPY: Goal.

MARCUS: Cha Fret you a let de Ras Clart Man score him a get easy goal, me no why him a score me no had me sounds wit me punch me a dub, Fret.

FRET: Him a lucky, him a lucky.

Goes, punches Juke Box (Reggae).
Throughout the later games music is
played.

ZIPPY: Lucky me Ras Clart dat a skill, skill from above, skill from Jah.

MARCUS: Jah, me Ras, wha you no bout Jah, dat a luck.

ZIPPY: Me no Jah, me talk ter Jah, him talk ter me, me an him communicate him a tell me hit de Ras Clart ball square, me hit it square it a go in square.

MARCUS: Cha.

ZIPPY: Me an Dole, we hand guided wha yer say Dole?

DOLE: Cha, him a seek him revenge.

MARCUS: Him a right me a hit yer Ras wid de Rod a Correction come Fret, block him Ras.

They play.

DOLE: Go way, go way yer Ras.

ZIPPY: Block him, block him Ras Clart.

MARCUS: Go in, go in, go, go.

ZIPPY: Block in, cha him gone.

MARCUS: Block him break Fret, Fret, block him, cross.

FRET: We have him de Fret ter Ras.

MARCUS: Good him Ras worry now, go in, go in.

ZIPPY: Dole.

MARCUS: Goal, goal ter Ras.

ZIPPY: Dole you let de Ras Clart Man jinx yer.

MARCUS: Whey yer communicate wid Jah gone me just cut yer wires. Jah do' want ter no you him a have better Ras Clart ting ter do.

ZIPPY: Aright one all.

MARCUS: Dat goal was scored by de Lion of Judea, de warrior of Redemption ter Ras Clart, me no me should have me dub.

ZIPPY: Make we play. Make we play.

MARCUS: Fret like him in a hurry ter buy Coke, him feeling rich come, Resurrection is at hand all Hypocrites I will shed blood come to Canaan.

They play.

ZIPPY: Block him Ras.

DOLE: Me block im.

ZIPPY: Up, up.

MARCUS: Me have it, me have it.

ZIPPY: Have me Ras, dey.

MARCUS: Me have it.

ZIPPY: Take him Dole.

DOLE: Me have im, him gone.

MARCUS: Fret him coming.

FRET: Me have im.

ZIPPY: Have dat yer Ras.

MARCUS: Fret.

ZIPPY: Goal, goal, fer Ras.

MARCUS: Cha Fret you let de Man walk round yer.

FRET: Me stop him.

MARCUS: Him score Man.

ZIPPY: Two one, yer see Jah will guide him servant to Paradise him will guide him Warrior ter wreck vengence on dose who face Judgement, de Sword of Jah is sharp and swift, wit love on one side an blood on de odder.

MARCUS: Judgement me Ras we have two more ter come we a go see who have Judgement.

ZIPPY: Righteousness is mine to give said Jah, you a get him punishment him wrath.

MARCUS: Shut yer Bomba.

DOLE: Make we play him, don't believe him have ter see yer him ter believe, him a unbeliever, him one a dem who have ter feel him pain.

They play.

MARCUS: Watch im Fret.

FRET: Me see im.

ZIPPY: See, im, yer could see Lightning yer could see de Desert Wind, see dat.

MARCUS: Good Fret.

FRET: Me see him Ras me read him like Genesis, Chapter One.

ZIPPY: Block him Dole.

MARCUS: Judgement come to him deserving.

DOLE: Me have him.

MARCUS: Have Ras.

ZIPPY: Watch im Dole, him wait.

DOLE: Me have im Ras covered.

MARCUS: Cover dat yer Heathen.

DOLE: Me have im.

MARCUS: Cover dat yer Hypocrite.

DOLE: Me cover im.

MARCUS: Cover dat yer Pagan.

DOLE: Me . . .

MARCUS: Goal, goal.

ZIPPY: Dole, him . . .

MARCUS: Him wat him cover dats wat him do, him conquer all Jericho is dats wat him do, eh Fret?

FRET: Cha.

MARCUS: Make we show one unbelievers who take de road ter greed an vanity dat rudeness do' pay, Cha me could taste de Ras Clart Coke already.

ZIPPY: Last game, two all.

DOLE: Him a make himself, Ras lose make him see.

MARCUS: Me a want one large glass ter Ras Clart, wid big ice an a straw, eh Fret?

FRET: Cha, dem a miss, dem goal.

ZIPPY: Aright make we see.

They play.

ZIPPY: Watch im Dole.

DOLE: Me have him.

MARCUS: Have . . . Fret him come.

FRET: Me have him.

ZIPPY: Have Bomba, him come Dole.

MARCUS: Dole a sleep ter Ras, me a shepherd.

MARCUS: Me a once walk round him.

DOLE: Me have him.

ZIPPY: Him a want ter sneak in, like Judas.

MARCUS: Judas me Ras, me a son of Jah, yer Hypocrite, take im Fret.

FRET: Me have im Ras.

ZIPPY: Have dat yer Ras.

FRET: Me tell yer me have him him path block im power miss.

MARCUS: Give him Judgement ter Ras.

ZIPPY: Dole im . . .

MARCUS: Judgement come.

ZIPPY: Him try Dole, block him.

MARCUS: Goal, goal, in yer Ras Clart, yer Bomba Clart, yer tink yer could escape de Sword of Correction you Hypocrite, Jah a say all will succumb, an him word is law.

ZIPPY: Dole you let dis Ras Clart beat we, Cha.

DOLE: Him lucky, Man.

MARCUS: Me no beat yer me righteousness beat yer, Cha Fret, dem a Ras Clart, en no de Warriors of Haile Selassie de Lion of Judah, de Lord of Lords de King of Kings, wen dem see him.

He beats his chest.

FRET: Whey de Coke dem, me a tirsty, all yer a deal Coke.

MARCUS: Cha yea, me a hot too, me a want me nice cool down make me gather me wisdom, ter confront dem Hypocrites, get dem Cokes.

ZIPPY: Make we wait till Sandy a come.

MARCUS: De Coke behind de Bar Man.

ZIPPY: Sandy have de keys Man.

MARCUS: Cha go behind de Bar and break him Ras, Man, me want me Coke.

ZIPPY: Nar Man.

MARCUS: Whey Sandy?

ZIPPY: She upstairs in de office.

MARCUS: Well call she down ter Ras, like yer want me break de Ras Clart lock or yer do' want ter pay fer yer sins.

ZIPPY: Me a pay, me a pay, Dole give Sandy a call.

DOLE: Cha make dem call, she na drink dem, Jah say, 'Make men toil fer him rewards', me do' like asking she Ras fer notting.

ZIPPY: Call de Ras Clart woman nar.

MARCUS: Cha me go call she nar fraid no Hypocrite me power stronger dan dem.(*He goes to the bottom of the stairs, shouts:*) Hey Sandy.

SANDY (*from upstairs*): What?

MARCUS: Come an open de Bar. Zippy want some Coke.

SANDY: I'm on the phone, hang on a minute.

MARCUS (*to the boys*): She a on de phone. Phone me Ras, dis place suppose ter be fer we, ter keep we outa danger, an you suppose ter be running dis place ter look after we, so come an do yer Ras Clart job. Wha de Ras Clart yer doing on de phone, making date for.

SANDY: I'm not making dates, give me a minute.

MARCUS: Me give you more den a Ras Clart minute, me box yer Ras Clart head. Cha if yer do' want ter interrupt yer romantic conversation trow down dem keys den, we go open up take four cokes an send back dem keys.

DOLE: Yea.

The others laugh.

SANDY: No.

MARCUS: Well come down or else me break him Ras Clart.

SANDY: Coming.

MARCUS: She a come, a no wat a bring she, Ras –

They laugh.
SANDY *comes downstairs. She is white, thirty to thirty-five, plump. She wears glasses, a long Indian skirt and a T-shirt and keys and a crucifix on a chain round her neck.*

SANDY: What's all the fuss about? I told you I was on the phone. It wouldn't of killed you to wait a minute, just for a few cokes, which are only going to rot your guts anyway. I told you.

MARCUS: We like Coke.

SANDY: You boys have no consideration. I was on the phone trying to find out what time Jacko's train gets in.

DOLE: Yer coulda fling down dem keys.

SANDY: You know that's not allowed, I'm responsible for them.

DOLE: Cha.

SANDY: You can Cha all you like, but what's the point in locking something if you don't keep the keys for it.

ZIPPY: Locks could get break.

SANDY: Yes, I know locks could be broken, so could doors and chairs and tables, and windows and I can go on for a month, but you know, don't you, so I won't but the whole purpose of having a lock is to make sure some one is responsible for the key, and that is why I have it. If the lock is broken that is not my responsibility.

MARCUS: So we could break the lock.

SANDY: I did not say that you know, you all know that. That is the last lock I am replacing. I've told you if that lock gets broken, you will have to go to the corner for your cokes. I mean it. I'm not going to keep up this farce.

DOLE: But dis a Youth Club, suppose ter have coke, I no some Youth Club have not only coke but orange, and food.

ZIPPY: Yea.

MARCUS: Me no an dat have Billiards an even Machine fer French Letter.

SANDY: Yes, I'm sure you do, I know of some that even have sensible boys who take part in activities and protect their centre and do repairs and paint also.

They laugh.

Yes, crazy as it may sound, they even feel proud of the centre so don't you start telling me about orange and Johnny machines. We've had all that and what happened? Someone was always putting money in and the machine was always jamming and someone always had to have a refund.

ZIPPY: De machine did jam.

SANDY: And who had to hand out the refund? Me.

MARCUS: Well you responsible.

SANDY: And when the engineers came, could we find the jammed coins, no they disappeared.

ZIPPY: It jammed.

SANDY: And what happened when someone broke open the machine? Did you all go and put those packets to some use to the good use they were designed specifically for? No. I wish to god you had.

ZIPPY: You leave Jah out of dis kind a talk.

SANDY: Oh I see I'm not allowed to have my God am I? Why? O.K. don't tell me I know. I am white, and we white people don't have a god, we don't believe in a god, we are devils. Is that right?

MARCUS: Cha, yer right, all a believe in money an greed an oppression, all yer oppress people.

SANDY: I see, and we are not oppressed as well. Look at me. I am as oppressed as you, more I think. I've got to worry about this place, to make sure it's run and keep it open, and clean and keep writing letters begging for money so that you harmless creatures have a quiet life, so that you good little boys keep out of trouble and so that I don't have to spend all my life in court saying 'Your Lordship he's never been in trouble before. I have found him responsible and sensible, and no I cannot put up the bail for him but I'm sure if you give him a suspended sentence he will have learned his lesson.' That is my oppression and I feel it so don't you tell me about oppression. Back to the Johnnies, those Johnnies you wanted. What did you do with them? You blew them up and strung them up on the ceiling didn't . . .

ZIPPY: We . . .

SANDY: Yes, you did, and you thought it was a big joke, when the girls came in didn't you?

MARCUS: Dem no wat Johnny look like.

The boys laugh.

SANDY: Yes, yes very funny they were upset and insulted I know that. You know what it told them, it told them you did not respect them, that they, black women, had not earned the respect of you their men. They didn't say it, but I saw their faces, and I also was insulted, me a white woman, I was also insulted. Are you surprised they don't want to come back? How many discos have we had?

DOLE: Two.

SANDY: And how many girls came.

DOLE: Not much.

SANDY: You see.

DOLE: But dem do' like heavy music, dem want soul, and all that funky business, dem en want Rasta music.

SANDY: The music has nothing to do with it, it's this place. We have got the worst name as far as centres go and that's saying something.

MARCUS: Dat en true you is a hypocrite me no places wid worse name den here, where wen one crowd inside de rest have ter pay dem money fer dem ter get inside.

SANDY: Yes all right we are perfect, one bright peaceful, little family.

ZIPPY: Hey Sandy, yer like dem Johnnys.

The boys laugh.

SANDY: No love they're for little boys like you to try an inflate.

MARCUS: Cha she call him little boy.

The boys laugh. Not ZIPPY.

DOLE: Sandy, wat inflate mean?

SANDY: It means to try to make yourself larger than you are.

DOLE: I taught dat was erection.

The boys laugh.

SANDY: No love, that is trying to make yourself smaller than you are. All right now how many cokes and who's paying.

ZIPPY: Marcus.

MARCUS: Nar Zippy.

ZIPPY: Nar Marcus.

MARCUS: Zippy Ras him lost me but, him carry him lost so him pay, ask Fret.

FRET: Him right.

SANDY: Now look, I don't care who's paying but I'm not unlocking that door until I see some money. I haven't got all day to waste here whilst you decide . . .

ZIPPY: All right here.

He gives her a pound.

Wha happen yer no joke?

SANDY: I'm sorry Zippy. Yes I joke. How many?

ZIPPY: Four. Make it five if ye want one.

SANDY: Thanks.

MARCUS: Watch im Sandy, he a try ter catch yer.

ZIPPY: Do' mind him. Catch wat? Me like Sandy, she no dat.

MARCUS: Yer see.

SANDY: I see I'll watch him. I think he's a nice boy. He's the only one of you who's offered to buy me a coke, that's for sure.

MARCUS: Is him lose him have ter pay.

SANDY (*taking the cokes to the table*): Nevertheless thanks all the same for the drink Zippy. I'm sure you would have bought even if you had won. Who beat who then?

MARCUS: Me an Fret lick dem Ras.

SANDY: Ah I didn't know you played Fret.

MARCUS: Me teach him, once an we lick dem me could teach anybody ter lick dem, dem no good.

SANDY: I see, so you're our champion.

ZIPPY: Champion wat, him is champion.

MARCUS: Me lick dem me an Fret.

DOLE: Do' mind he Sandy, he a make one set a noise him put me off.

ZIPPY: Yes him just lucky.

MARCUS: Luck, me Ras, me give dem all me powers of righteousness, Rasta Man en depend on luck, all him a have is him righteousness. Right Sandy?

SANDY: Right, you'll have to play against Jacko when he comes to see who is the real champ.

MARCUS: Him good?

SANDY: He was our champion.

ZIPPY: Whey him is?

SANDY: He was inside and he's coming out today.

She looks at her watch.

He's out. He's on the way home

and I've got to meet him at the station at half-three.

MARCUS: Wat him went in fer.

SANDY: He's a nice guy you guys will like him and yes, that's something I wanted to say. When he comes he's going to be feeling a bit strange so no aggro.

MARCUS: We do' give aggro.

SANDY: You know what I mean.

MARCUS: No.

SANDY: Come on.

MARCUS: Cha all right. Wat him like, him a Rasta?

SANDY: No I don't think so. I don't know he's been inside for . . .

DOLE: How long him get.

SANDY: Nine years.

DOLE: Dat long?

SANDY: Yes.

DOLE: Dem barstard. Wen dem lock up blackman dem make sure him lock up long.

ZIPPY: Wat him get lock fer?

SANDY: Rape; he and three boys.

ZIPPY: An him get catch, him en rape good.

The boys laugh.

SANDY: Very funny.

ZIPPY: Me never rape, but if me rape me go rape so good no girl en go get Police, she a go want more an more.

The boys laugh.

SANDY: Now stop that. That is not funny. That's what you and a lot of men think. That's why so many women are raped and so many men and boys – boys like you and Jacko – are sent to prison. No, it is not funny, I'm sorry, no man has any right to rape a woman, no matter what his reasons are or what he thinks she wants, you hear, and it's not funny. Jacko took part or the girl said he took part.

MARCUS: Dem girl tell lie dem is Hypocrite.

SANDY: All right and she recognised him, she knew him.

ZIPPY: An she inform on him?

SANDY: Yes.

ZIPPY: Him no rape good me say.

The boys laugh.

SANDY: I said it wasn't funny.

ZIPPY: Me bet yer it was one white girl, dem Ras Clart, always want ter pretend dem good.

SANDY: How much.

ZIPPY: Wat?

SANDY: How much you'd like to bet?

ZIPPY: Why?

SANDY: How much you want to bet it was a white girl, because I'd bet you.

MARCUS: It was a black girl.

SANDY: That's right. Why do you think it was a white girl?

MARCUS: I didn't say it was a white girl, it's him.

SANDY: It's him I'm talking to. Eh Zippy why, you don't think black girls are sexy too?

ZIPPY: No, black girls sexy, me like black girls.

SANDY: So you think white girls should get raped.

ZIPPY: No, me never say dat, but dem like boys ter gang dem an wen dem finish an dem realise wat happen, dem start ter feel ashamed and say it happen widout dem consent, me see dem in de back a disco, plenty, if me wanted to me coulda just walk up an . . .

SANDY: All right Zippy and you know why? It's because young girls go there, and they have something to drink. Something like whisky which they can't or shouldn't drink and that's what happens.

ZIPPY: Dem like it.

SANDY: Would you like –

ZIPPY: No me tell yer me never do it.

SANDY: No, I mean would you like five men to . . .

ZIPPY: Me like five women.

The boys laugh.

SANDY: All right, very funny.

MARCUS: Do' mind dat Zippy, Sandy. Tell me beat dis champion, me want ter no all bout him, him strategy, how me go lick him, him does flick or him does stroke.

SANDY: Both, sorry Marcus I don't know much about it, but he was always winning.

MARCUS: All him games?

SANDY: Yes, he used to teach . . .

MARCUS: Cha, him a cheat.

SANDY: No, Marcus.

MARCUS: No man car win all him games, you a miss . . . so him a Warrior me go have ter watch him.

SANDY: Yes, Marcus.

DOLE: Him lost one game an him get five.

MARCUS: If him so cool Sandy how come him get catch ter Ras.

SANDY: He didn't get caught, I told you the girl remembered him and told the Police, and he refused to give the other boy's name so . . .

MARCUS: Cha.

DOLE: Yes.

MARCUS: Cha him a genuine warrior ter Ras.

SANDY: Call him wat you like just try and be nice to him when he comes he's bound to feel a bit . . . just try.

MARCUS: All right Cha.

SANDY looks at her watch.

SANDY: I better leave now or else I'll miss him.

MARCUS: Sandy wat about dem robes yer was making fer me.

SANDY: You want them now?

MARCUS: Yes, we must look like proper Rasta, to greet de warrior.

SANDY: All right, they're in my office on the floor behind the cabinet. Now look I'm leaving you in charge Marcus.

MARCUS: Wid de keys.

SANDY: Oh – No, you don't need them.

MARCUS: We might need some cokes.

SANDY: I won't be that long. Christ I almost forgot.

MARCUS: Leave Jah out of dis.

SANDY: Listen there's a girl coming here she was meant to be here by two but she's late so tell her I won't be long, will you.

MARCUS: Who's she?

SANDY: My new helper or warden, whichever you like, and don't give her a hard time, practise being nice on her so that when Jacko comes you'll be perfect, we don't want her to get the right impression on her first day do we?

MARCUS: Wat?

SANDY: Never mind just be nice to her for my sake. Right keys yes, gloves in the car, yes, right, I'm off. Be good.

She smiles and goes.

MARCUS: Cha, me in charge a wat dis Ras Clart place, en worth notting she no give me no keys so how me a in charge, she a hypocrite Man genuine hypocrite dat.

ZIPPY: Marcus make me get dem robes Nar.

MARCUS: Cha why yer ask me.

ZIPPY: You are General.

MARCUS: Cha me no General if yer want robes go find dem yerself, come Fret make me get some practice, before me face dis Goliath.

FRET *and* MARCUS *go to the football machine. They play.*

ZIPPY: Dole make we go upstairs get we robes.

DOLE: Cha me do' want no robes Man, me a stay here, fight ya.

ZIPPY: Cha.

He goes upstairs.

DOLE: Hey Marcus, you a practise yer Ras you still en go beat nobody.

MARCUS: Shut yer Ras me beat you, me beat you an Zippy, yer no hear wat Sandy a say? She say me champion.

DOLE: Champion wat? Champion caretaker? She a left you in charge a de broom ter Ras.

MARCUS: Shut yer mouth, Bomba

hypocrite, you a interfere wid de working a Jah.

DOLE: Jah me Ras, you a scheming to beat one guy, de guy out a practice, him been put away for five year, you a want to outnumber de poor guy you en no genuine warrior you a Herod ter Ras.

MARCUS: Shut yer mouth before me box yer Ras.

ZIPPY *comes down in an African robe.*

ZIPPY: Cha, me a genuine Ethiopian now me a warrior of de Lion, ter Ras Clart, all yer a see Rasta ter Ras Heavy Cloth.

MARCUS: Cha you look good boy.

ZIPPY: Me look genuine no hypocrite ting dis a genuine robe.

MARCUS: Whey we own?

ZIPPY: Dem a upstairs.

MARCUS: Cha.

He runs upstairs followed by DOLE. FRET *walks. Sounds from upstairs.*

Cha, give me dat.

ZIPPY *(jumping, sings):* By de waters of Babylon . . .Cha

A girl, GAIL, *enters. She is black, attractive (twenty to twenty-five) and is wearing a jacket, skirt and jumper.*

GAIL: Hello.

ZIPPY: Yes.

GAIL: I came to see Sandy.

ZIPPY: Yes, she a gone out but she left a message she say she en go be long ter wait fer she.

GAIL: Yes, I'm a bit late I couldn't find the place.

ZIPPY: Yes, Cha take a seat she a come soon.

GAIL *(sits)*: Thank you, it looks nice.

ZIPPY: It aright it have office upstairs you ar want to see it.

GAIL: No I better wait till Sandy comes.

ZIPPY: Yea, you a come ter work?

GAIL: I hope so, it's up to Sandy if she likes me.

ZIPPY: Cha, Sandy cool she a like you she a like everybody, you en help she out.

GAIL: Yes.

ZIPPY: Wat you a do?

GAIL: I . . . Lots of things, try to keep you busy most of all. Are you the only one here?

ZIPPY: No de rest a guys upstairs dey look fer dem robes, you like it? *(Stands.)* It a genuine Ethiopian robe.

GAIL: Yes, it's very nice.

ZIPPY: Sandy a make dem fer we. She a cool, you a ask she, she make you one.

GAIL: Yes, I'll ask her, so what other rooms do you have.

ZIPPY: Cha, not much we a have office an phone upstairs, toilet over dey.

GAIL: One?

ZIPPY: Nar two, one for de girls.

GAIL: Yes.

ZIPPY: An in de back dey it a have a room for discos.

GAIL: Ah, I like dancing, how often do you . . .

ZIPPY: Cha, not too often, it a some time one week, some time two weeks, not steady. Whey you from?

GAIL: London.

ZIPPY: But yer people black.

GAIL: Yes.

ZIPPY: Cha, me no dat me take one look at yer me no yer people a dem black. You is a Rastafarian?

GAIL: No, I don't think so, not that I have anything against it, I just don't know anything about it.

ZIPPY: Me tell yer, me explain everything not Marcus him a hypocrite.

GAIL: Who's Marcus?

ZIPPY: Him a upstairs. Yer see Rastafarian is a Man who believe in de Bible all peace an love an him a believe in Emperor Haile Selassie to be de Lion a Judah de King of Kings and Lord of Lords.

GAIL: Yes?

ZIPPY: Dat is something eh, dat is Rasta Man, him belief. Yes, an all white people all a dem, dem a genuine hypocrite dem.

GAIL: Yes I see.

ZIPPY: See dat wat Rasta man believe.

GAIL: And you're a Rasta Man?

ZIPPY: Cha all a we a Rasta an all Rasta Man believe in him dread locks.

GAIL: Yes, the hair.

ZIPPY: Dat not him hair, dat him dread locks.

GAIL: I see, so tell me what sort of things you do here?

ZIPPY: Cha me nar do much, we a play some dominoes, some football, some sounds.

GAIL: You have a team?

ZIPPY: Nar, over dey.

GAIL: Yes. What else?

ZIPPY: Fool around, talk.

GAIL: Ah, what do you talk about?

ZIPPY: All kinda ting, Rastafarian tings, an Ethopia.

GAIL: Would you all like to go to Africa?

ZIPPY: Sure all a we want go dey some day.

GAIL: Good, well maybe we could go on a trip to see some exhibits from Africa.

ZIPPY: Where?

GAIL: In London, there's always something going on concerning Africa, you'd be surprised.

ZIPPY: But dat not Africa dat a white man ting, dem a hypocrite, dem not genuine Africa, is Africa we want ter see, we want ter see real Lion not dem Circus ting.

GAIL: I see, but it would give you some idea, of what life is really like in Africa.

ZIPPY: Cha, but not Africa, we want ter no we in Africa dats what we want ter no, you a see.

GAIL: Yes, where are you from?

ZIPPY: Me from Jamaica?

GAIL: You were born in Jamaica?

ZIPPY: No, we born in London, but me people from Jamaica.

GAIL: But you speak with a Jamaican . . .

ZIPPY: Cha, me could talk London if me

wanted too but me is a Rastafarian so me talk Ja.

GAIL: I see.

ZIPPY: Yer all genuine Rasta Man him a talk Jamaican or else him not genuine.

GAIL: Yes, and all the other boys they were born in London.

ZIPPY: Some a dem born in Jamaica some born in London me do' no.

GAIL: Are they allowed to be upstairs so long?

ZIPPY: Cha Sandy she a cool, she left Marcus in charge. Him upstairs. You a want to see him we call im fer you.

GAIL: No. (*She gets up.*) I'll just look around. (*She looks at a poster.*)

ZIPPY: Dat is de Emperor Haile Selassie.

GAIL: Yes.

ZIPPY: You no him face?

GAIL: Yes.

ZIPPY: Cha, you is Rastafarian.

GAIL: Are women allowed to be Rastafarian.?

ZIPPY: Cha yes Man all black people is Rastafarian. Is wat dem believe.

GAIL: I see you have a bar.

ZIPPY: Yes.

GAIL: Do you run it yourselves?

ZIPPY: Nar Sandy, it a only keep coke.

GAIL: Would you like to run it yourselves?

ZIPPY: Cha wat for, it enmake no profit, it fer someting ter drink, it do' need no running.

MARCUS, DOLE *and* FRET *come down in robes.*

MARCUS: Cha Zippy a pick up chick.

ZIPPY: Me no pick up no chick Ras dis Gail come to help out Sandy.

GAIL: Hello, I'm Gail.

MARCUS: Yes me no, Gail Roberts.

GAIL: How did you know, have we met?

MARCUS: No me no yer name, Sandy a tell me yer come an ter take care a you, she left me in charge, me name is Marcus, me was named after de great black warrior Marcus Garvey.

GAIL: Yes, . . .

MARCUS: Dis is Dole, cause since him born him a draw dole an dis is Fret, him is my warrior an him do Fret.

GAIL: I see. Hello. Your friend was telling me all the good things you do here.

MARCUS: Who Zippy? Him do' no notting, me is in charge, me running ting, Sandy say fer me ter look after you not Zippy.

GAIL: Well he was the one I met first and –

MARCUS: Cha, yer shoulda wait fer me, me in charge.

ZIPPY: Do' take no notice a he yer no him just want ter prove him point, him didn't want to be in no command.

MARCUS: Cha shut yer Ras mouth.

GAIL: It's okay, I'm fine. How long is Sandy going to be?

MARCUS: She a back soon, she gone to get a guy him Jacko.

GAIL: Oh yes, who's Jacko? I see you're having a party for him.

MARCUS: It no party him a coming out today dat all, him a Sandy friend.

GAIL: I see.

MARCUS: You a work here?

GAIL: I hope so. I was saying to Zippy I hope I can organise some outings and get you guys to come along.

MARCUS: Wat kind a outing? Ter Museum an ting?

GAIL: No, I thought maybe we could visit a Safari Park, and see the animals they have. Lions and tigers.

MARCUS: Me do' want ter see no Sarfari Park, Sarfari is a white man ting dat a fer white people, in dem car to visit.

GAIL: I just thought maybe you might like to see some lions.

MARCUS: Cha me no wat lions look like.

GAIL: Or maybe a factory or something.

MARCUS: Factory wat, wat kinda factory?

GAIL: Any kind of factory where they make things. We could see how its done.

MARCUS: Wat?

GAIL: Anything. I have a friend who works for a record studio. We could maybe go and see how they make records, see how its done. You like music?

MARCUS: Me like Reggae. Heavy Dub. Who him a cut?

GAIL: They cut all kind of records there. Maybe we could go when they are doing some Reggae.

MARCUS (calls out): Hey all yer hear dat, dis girl no people who make reggae record.

GAIL: A friend.

DOLE: Cha, dat good.

MARCUS: She a take we ter see.

GAIL: I could try and arrange it.

MARCUS: Cha you cool, me dig dat.

GAIL: What other sort of things do you like? Sports?

MARCUS: Yer mean running in dem shorts.

GAIL: Yes.

MARCUS: Nar, cha, dem a school boy ting. Me like chick and me disco.

GAIL: I see.

MARCUS: Me like Rasta man ting.

GAIL: Yes Zippy was explaining to me.

MARCUS: Him no explain notting. Him no genuine rasta man. Him is real hypocrite. Is me de rasta man here. Anyting you want to no bout rasta man you ask me. Me no all bout Ethiopia.

GAIL: And Haile Selassie.

MARCUS: Him to him is de King of Kings Lord of –

GAIL: Lords.

MARCUS: You no him?

GAIL: Yes.

MARCUS: Dis friend wit him record studio him yer boyfriend?

GAIL: How did you know it was a him?

MARCUS: Me no, me no dem tings, me is a righteous man, an me righteousness tell me dem ting, it tell me all kinda ting, me no yer name was Roberts before anybody.

GAIL: He's a friend yes.

MARCUS: Boyfriend.

GAIL: Friend.

MARCUS: Wat kinda friend?

GAIL: A sort of friend.

MARCUS: A sort of boyfriend?

GAIL: A sort of friend.

MARCUS: Wat sort?

GAIL: A sort, any sort really. You have friends.

MARCUS: You mean like me an Fret?

GAIL: Is Fret your boyfriend?

MARCUS: Cha shut yer ras clart mouth.

GAIL: I'm sorry.

MARCUS: Me is genuine rasta man, rasta man do have no boyfriend dat is white man ting.

GAIL: I said I was sorry it was a joke.

MARCUS: Cha, me nearly box yer face if Sandy did ask me look after you me box. Rasta Man don't do dem kinda tings, da is hypocrite ting.

GAIL: I'm sorry (*She takes out a cigarette.*) Would you like a cigarette?

MARCUS: Me no smoke tobacco me smoke Ganja, rasta man he smoke no tobacco.

GAIL: Look I'm really sorry, it was a joke right? O.K. a bad one, O.K. . . .

MARCUS: Cha.

He walks off and joins the others. He says something. They laugh.
ZIPPY *comes over to* GAIL.

GAIL: Hi.

ZIPPY: Hi.

GAIL: I think I upset your friend.

ZIPPY: Who, Marcus? Do' mind him him a have big mouth dats all him have.'

GAIL: Yes, but all the same I think maybe I shouldn't have.

ZIPPY: Do' mind him, him just want to prove him is big man dats him problem.

GAIL: Yes a lot of men have that problem.

I think I'll go upstairs and wait in the office.

ZIPPY: Yer want me show yer?

GAIL: No thanks.

ZIPPY: It right at de top a de stairs, make yer self at home.

GAIL: Thanks.

She goes.
MARCUS *comes to* ZIPPY.
Music.

MARCUS: Cha, punch me a dub dey . . . Cha whey she a gone?

ZIPPY: She gone upstairs ter wait for Sandy.

MARCUS: Me do' no if she fer wait in office.

ZIPPY: Cha shut yer mouth, Sandy say look after she, you a give she one get a heavy sound. Wha rang wit yer? Yer brainy, or wat? De chick is a nice chick, man.

MARCUS: She a hypocrite, me nearly box she face.

ZIPPY: Box me Ras, you not boxing nobody face.

MARCUS: Who go stop me?

ZIPPY: Me, me and de lion of Ethiopia to stop yer cha, you like ter go en wit dis ras clart ting too long, me vex now, me vex, me spirit go an get vex now ras clart, me no heavy guy yer no but wen me get vex, me vex, Cha, go way Duck me ter ras –

ZIPPY walks off, goes in the corner and sits.

MARCUS: All right, brother man me duck yer.

MARCUS goes to the boys.
SANDY enters with JACKO.
JACKO is tall (twenty to twenty-five). He is wearing a suit and tie.

SANDY: Hi everybody, this is Jacko come and say hello.

ZIPPY goes and shakes his hand.

ZIPPY: Hi man.

DOLE (*slaps his hand*): Hi.

MARCUS: Hey brother how yer is?

FRET comes.

FRET: Hi.

SANDY: His train was late and I got held up, so how's things? What's been happening? I see everything's still in one piece.

MARCUS: We had some cokes.

SANDY *goes to the bar.*

SANDY: Oh no, I warned you I warned ... (*Looks.*) Shit Marcus I must be stupid you get me every time, don't you? I never learn, it's my trusting nature. O.K. you guys relax. Take a seat Jacko, you're no stranger.

JACKO: Tanks.

SANDY: And the place hasn't changed that much, some paint here and there that's all, so make yourself at home.

JACKO: It feels good.

SANDY: That's because it's home.

ZIPPY: Sandy that girl come.

SANDY: Christ and what happened?

ZIPPY: She upstairs, waiting.

SANDY: Christ, O.K. I'll go and see her. You, look (*Gives the keys to* ZIPPY.) open the box, let's all have some cokes, I'll get her.

She goes upstairs.
ZIPPY *goes behind the bar and brings out some cokes.*

MARCUS: Hey look Zippy nar him is now Barman in Hotel.

ZIPPY *opens coke and gives one to* JACKO.

ZIPPY: Here brother man try dis.

JACKO: Tanks.

ZIPPY: All yer help all yer ras.

SANDY *and* GAIL *come down.*

SANDY: Have you met everybody?

GAIL: Yes.

SANDY: But you haven't met Jacko. This is Jacko.

GAIL: Hello Jacko.

JACKO: Hello.

SANDY: Oh I'm sorry Gail, it is Gail isn't it?

GAIL: Yes.

SANDY: Let's have a coke then, I'm paying for the damn things.

She takes one for GAIL, *gives it to her. She looks at* JACKO.

Oh you've got one. All right everybody, to Jacko, welcome home Jacko.

They all repeat this. They drink.
SANDY *sits.*

Right let's relax now, I needed this. (*The coke.*) I've been rushing all day. First it was you and I had to get Jacko, and I haven't stopped. So come on then tell me what you think of us.

GAIL: I think you're all nice, great.

SANDY: Well I wouldn't go that far, but we're all right. Let's say we're not as bad as we appear.

GAIL: O.K.

SANDY: So what do you think? You think you'd like to work with us?

GAIL: Yes, I think so.

SANDY: Great, hey everybody, Gail is going to work with us.

ZIPPY *goes and shakes* GAIL's *hand.*

ZIPPY: Yea, welcome sister.

SANDY: That's the spirit. Anybody else?

MARCUS: Cha.

The others wave.

SANDY: Take no notice, they're all rushing to welcome you. Lets drink to Gail.

They drink to GAIL.

GAIL: Thank you. What do I have to do?

SANDY: We'll talk about it, it's not much. Things like answer the phone, take messages, be in charge here when I go out, which is going to be more often I hope. Those sort of things, oh yes, and any bright ideas you have for keeping these guys occupied, except dominoes, the Juke Box or football; we've got those.

GAIL: I noticed.

SANDY: Yes. Now, we're not much of a candidate for Youth Club of the year.

GAIL: We'll make it better. When can I start?

SANDY: Right now. Come upstairs, I'll show you what's what and what goes where.

GAIL: Great.

SANDY: O.K. you guys look after Jacko, and don't let them cheek you Jacko.

JACKO: I'm all right.

SANDY: Come on then.

SANDY *is on the stairs.*

ZIPPY: Hey Sandy how yer like dem robes.

SANDY: Great, they look genuine.

SANDY *and* GAIL *go up.*

ZIPPY: Cha, hey brother how yer like dem robes.

JACKO: Dey look nice.

ZIPPY: If yer ask Sandy she a make yer one too.

JACKO: Wat dey for? All yer doing a show or wat?

ZIPPY: Show, no man, ras dis is genuine Ethiopian robes, we is rasta man, genuine rasta man yer do no bout rastafarian?

JACKO: No not much.

ZIPPY: Cha me forget you been lock up for long time, well rastafarian is black man ting now we discover we identity is rastafarian dats it.

JACKO: I hear bout it in Jamaica long time.

ZIPPY: Well it a come ter Britain now, we call it Babylon da is Britain so tell me brother man wat it like inside de man place, fer how long?

JACKO: Five years.

ZIPPY: Wat is a like?

JACKO: It's not bad, as long as you follow de rules.

ZIPPY: Follow dem rules me no follow nobody rules.

JACKO: Well when yer inside dere yer have ter or else . . .

ZIPPY: Or else wat?

JACKO: Or else, dey make yer pay.

ZIPPY: Cha nobody car make me a do wat me do' want ter do.

JACKO: Well inside dey do, a only hope you don't have ter go in.

ZIPPY: Cha me nar go inside dem never catch me, me smarter dem all dem ras.

JACKO: O.K.

ZIPPY: But you is a warrior ter ras.

JACKO: How yer mean.

ZIPPY: Sandy she tell we. Sandy tell we how yer en give dem Babylon yer friend en dem names how yer no tell dem notting.

JACKO: Yes.

ZIPPY: Dats heroic ting man, dats wat genuine rasta man go do man.

JACKO: Yes.

ZIPPY: Genuine hero man even Sandy a call yer hero.

JACKO: Tanks, so wat you guys do all dey just come here?

ZIPPY: Cha yes is a good place man. Dis is de only place in dis town whey we could come an relax an en get no harrassment. We could do we own ting here, an dey en have nobody ter tell we wat ter do or asking we wat we doing. If we go by de corner, is Panda Car come up, ter ask we question, ras clart, dem do' like ter see we doing notting. Everybody must be doing someting, working or going somewhere or coming from somewhere. If dem see people relaxing dem tink dem up ter someting. Dem people do' relax so dem do' like ter see people relax. Dem like ter have heart attack an give people dem heart attack.

JACKO: Yes.

ZIPPY: Cha brother me like you me could make you genuine rasta man.

JACKO: I do' no, I do' no.

ZIPPY: Cha it no sweat you a catch yer spirit.

MARCUS *comes over.*

MARCUS: Hey brother man yer no how ter play dat game?

JACKO: Yes, ah used ter . . .

MARCUS: Come den nar, me give yer a game, make we play.

JACKO: All right.

He goes.

MARCUS: Hey Zippy you a come watch.

ZIPPY: Nar, Cha, go long.

JACKO *and* MARCUS *go to the football game.*

MARCUS: Make we toss fer kick off.

JACKO: All right.

Puts his hand in his pocket.

MARCUS: Me have coin, me have coin. (*Tosses.*) Head nor tail?

JACKO: Head.

MARCUS: Head a win, make we punch me tune . . .

Music.
JACKO *kicks off. They play.* DOLE *and* FRET *go to watch.*

MARCUS: Cha go in.

DOLE: Him block yer Marcus.

MARCUS: Shut yer Ras. Cha go in dat ras.

DOLE: Him cover yer ras Marcus.

JACKO: All yer take dis game serious.

MARCUS: Serious Ras it a warfare ter ras go in.

DOLE: You no about him ras Marcus him block all yer ras clart move. Look how him cool, him a real warrior him worry yer ras.

MARCUS: Worry who ras, me a righteous man. Righteous man no lose no contest.

DOLE: Win it den nar.

MARCUS: Cha go in, go in.

JACKO: Yer good man.

MARCUS: Cha course me a good, goodness breed goodness, go in.

DOLE: Him a block yer ras.

MARCUS: Block . . . goal, cha me win, me win.

JACKO: Good goal.

MARCUS: Goal ter ras me is now champion warrior, me win, all yer a see how righteousness does triumph over evil.

JACKO: Good game, da was a good goal. Yer want ter play another game?

MARCUS: Nar, nar me no play no more me win.

DOLE: But Marcus yer only win one game ter ras clart de rules . . .

MARCUS: De rules wat rules? Who makes rules? Me ras clart me win da is all. We no play.

DOLE: Dat en Justice man, de man rusty ter ras, him a just come out him not proficient him just a warm up.

JACKO: I do' mind.

ZIPPY: No him right.

MARCUS: Cha me do' defend no title, right away me get me crown first.

ZIPPY: Cha. (*Goes and sits. To* DOLE.) Leave him ras.

MARCUS: Me champ ter ras.

JACKO: All right, but a hope yer go give me another game.

MARCUS: Cha sure sure me give yer plenty game ter ras, all a dem go be like dat ter ras.

DOLE: Marcus you is not a righteous man, me say dat now, an me never change it, you is not righteous.

MARCUS: Cha, ne warrior you a ras clart hypocrite, wat you no, me have de blood of Haile Selassie an all dem great warrior a pumping in a veins, blood a true warrior cha. (*Sits with* FRET.)
DOLE *goes and sits with* ZIPPY.

DOLE: Dat man is a . . .

ZIPPY: Cha, left him ras.

DOLE: Brother man de mind dat ras him profess ter be genuine, but him crooked, him a take de wrong path, but him go learn, some heavy wisdom, wen him come ter me him maker. Do' let him attitude distort yer destiny, ter ras.

JACKO: Nar is all right. I no guys like him dey have guys like him inside, dey have ter be big, bigger dan everybody or have more dan everybody else.

DOLE: Him a Lazarus man, is him sores him want ter spread.

JACKO: If he went inside, he see how big he really was, one night a would give him.

DOLE: Wat it like inside brother man, it tough?

JACKO: Yes it tough, if you tink tings tough outside a prison, it ten time more tough inside, de white screws . . .

DOLE: De is de guards?

JACKO: Yes dem do' like yer at all an if yer black den is worse. Dey do' give yer a chance. Yer have ter ask dem fer everyting, everyting. An de white cons dem come next dem higher dan yer, dem have tings under control an yer have ter ask dem fer favours too. An every favour yer get yer have ter pay back wid interest, an yer car miss no excuse or yer pay more an more an den everyting yer do have a rule an regulations ter cover it. So all yer guys tink outside hard eh all yer do' no how easy it is . . . take my word fer it, I en going back inside. I make dat pledge de first night I spend, notting go get me inside again. I en care if a man killing me modder I go let him . . .

DOLE: Yer hear dat Zippy.

ZIPPY: Me hear.

DOLE: Like wat kinda tings dem do . . . ?

ZIPPY: Cha rest de man nar, yer en see de man en want ter talk . . .

JACKO: Nar is all right, I do' mind, I en mind talking bout it, is . . .

DOLE: Me hear dat is man does fock man.

JACKO: Yes.

DOLE: Me would never let no man get me.

ZIPPY: Cha.

DOLE: Me would kill him first.

JACKO: How much people yer could kill, ten, five, three?

DOLE: All a dem.

ZIPPY: Cha rest yer ras nar.

DOLE: Me kill all a dem, ras, me poison dem me choke dem me.

ZIPPY: Cha man go way wid dat ras nar.

JACKO: Yes.

DOLE: Aright, me stop.

SANDY *and* GAIL *come downstairs.*

SANDY: All right who missed me?

MARCUS: Me win Sandy, me win, me is now de reigning champion me beat yer Jacko licks.

SANDY: I see.

MARCUS: Me beat him.

SANDY: Is that true?

JACKO: Yes.

MARCUS: Me say it true yer no have ter ask, you now have ter put up one sign saying Marcus is reigning champion pon wall.

SANDY: All right Marcus, but I still don't believe it. Why don't you write the sign yourself? You'll find some card and the felt-tips upstairs.

MARCUS: Cha champion shouldn't have ter write his own sign.

SANDY: Yes Marcus, but you know exactly what you want to say and how it should look. Make it pretty, use lots of colours.

MARCUS: Cha yes, me use de colours of Ethiopia, de red de gold an de green ter ras.

SANDY: Yes.

MARCUS: All right, Cha all yer hypocrite do' no how ter say glorious ting.

SANDY: Why not do it now.

MARCUS: Cha.

SANDY: Dole run upstairs and get the card and pens for me.

DOLE: Me en going Cha make him go an get him.

SANDY: For me.

DOLE: Cha.

GAIL: I'll go. (*She moves.*)

SANDY: Thanks Gail.

SANDY *calls out to* GAIL.

SANDY: You'll find some in the cupboard.

MARCUS: Cha, dat is power of righteousness.

SANDY: That is downright laziness. I don't know why I put up with it. I must be stupid.

MARCUS: Cha you is a maiden at de Palace of King Marcus ter ras.

SANDY *goes to* JACKO *and* ZIPPY.

SANDY (*to* JACKO): How are we then, you O.K.?

JACKO: I'm cool.

SANDY: Zippy's looking after you then.

ZIPPY: Cha, me do' have ter look after nobody him a big man, him look after himself.

GAIL (*at the top of the stairs*): Sandy should I bring all the pens?

SANDY: Christ. (*Calls out.*) Yes bring them.

GAIL *comes down. She gives pens and card to* MARCUS.

GAIL: Here you are.

MARCUS: Tanks sister me go make you second hand maiden to me court.

GAIL: Do you want me to give you some ideas?

MARCUS: No tanks sister, me is one heavy designer wen we start ter use me righteous hand me goodness does come out, me do' need no hypocrite to guide me hand.

GAIL: I only . . .

MARCUS: Cha, me no yer went ter Art School an ting but me is a natural.

GAIL: How do you know, I did . . .

MARCUS: Me no everyting bout you sister me no yer background yer foreground yer cricket ground and yer football ground me no all bout you, me no yer people an dey respectable, an yer come from posh school.

GAIL: Not really.

MARCUS: Cha, yes really you a one English black woman, you a not one a we, you look genuine but me no bout you, every ting . . .

GAIL: Really?

MARCUS *starts to draw.*

MARCUS: Yes, me ask me guardian spirit bout you an him tell me everyting cha.

GAIL: Okay, but it's better if you do an outline sketch first.

She goes to ZIPPY, SANDY *and* JACKO. *She sits.*

GAIL: That guy is crazy.

SANDY: Who Marcus? No he's not, he's sweet and tender and kind and understanding and totally unselfish, but he's a lazy infuriating bastard. He'll tease the life out of you if you let him.

GAIL: He's doing it all ready. He knows so many things about me, I can't understand how he . . .

SANDY: He's got you worried has he?

GAIL: Yes, he . . . he makes me feel as though we've met before, but I know we haven't.

SANDY: That's Marcus, he's a cunning bastard. That's his best trick. He tries to undermine you and . . .

GAIL: Yes that's what he does and he's so good at it.

SANDY: You'll get used to it.

GAIL: I hope I don't, it's so scary.

SANDY: He's harmless, a bastard, but harmless.

ZIPPY: Cha him a want somebody put a stop ter his life, dat wat.

JACKO: No man, do' say dem ting, dat is trouble, guys like he always run away but dey leave you to answer for dem actions.

SANDY: Marcus is one of life's crosses that's all. We all have to bear him that's all. So (*To* GAIL:) you think you're ready to take over for a little while?

GAIL: Yes, sure.

SANDY: I've got to run Jacko over to his place.

GAIL: I'll be fine.

SANDY: Good I won't be long but you never know. Come on Jacko let's go. (*Rises.*) Now listen everybody, I'm going to take Jacko to his place and see him settled in, so I'm leaving Gail in charge. I won't be long, so if you need anything see Gail, O.K? Be good.

MARCUS: Cha, yer leaving she dem keys me bet.

SANDY: Thank you Marcus, I almost forgot. (*She takes the keys off her neck and gives them to* GAIL.) Don't let him eat you.

GAIL (*laughs*): Go on I'll be fine.

SANDY (*to all*): O.K. enjoy yourselves. Come on Jacko.

JACKO (*to all*): See you guys.

ZIPPY: Right, take care.

DOLE: Cool.

MARCUS: Cha.

JACKO *and* SANDY *leave.*

GAIL: O.K. I'll be upstairs if you need me.

She goes upstairs.

MARCUS: Cha me do' need she ras. Hey Dole how dis a sound in nineteen-seventy-nine in dis place me de warrior of de Lion of Judea Emperor Haile Selassie, Lord of Lords, King of Kings, defeated no conquered a fellow call Jacko who was de champion at football. Cha how yer like it?

DOLE: Like me ras, it a bomba.

MARCUS: Me no yer would like it ter ras, signed, who a go sign it, Dole?

DOLE: Sign it yer ras self.

MARCUS: Nar, me have ter have impartial Judge come beat witness, come nar Dole.

DOLE: Go way yer ras, ask Zippy.

ZIPPY: Cha.

MARCUS: Nar, Fret, nar nar Fret, Sandy me go get Sandy, me do' want no Corporal me go get General, me go get Sandy she a respectable, yes or me could get wat she name upstairs, Madame Roberts ter sign, wha yer a say ter dat eh Zippy?

ZIPPY: Cha why you do a rest de girl, de girl come here ter do she ting, yer keep up one set a ras, wat wrong wit yer man, yer keep up. Keep up dis ras so long.

MARCUS: Dis is part a she job, dis is what she a here for yer tink is like me like she Cha. Man is you a like she, you afraid me power a righteousness capture she eh?

ZIPPY: Yes, me like she no wat.

MARCUS: Me do' care, man. Me no dat dat is clear vision me get. Cha, pon she say if we a need she ter come, fer she me need she now, eh me a need yer baby.

ZIPPY: Cha, you a ras clart satan, you a want tempt somebody into some wilderness but you en go tempt me, you go tempt you ras self go dey, yer dey already cha.

DOLE: Whatap, good, blow Zippy, him never go recover dat spirit blow, him get him Rod of Correction. Cross him back ter ras.

MARCUS: Cha all yer a miss all all yer a blow miss because me is a genuine rasta no stone car touch me, me have de protection of Daniel, cha, all yer not even Lion. Fret go ask she fer me.

FRET: Wat?

MARCUS: Go ask she ter sign me record.

FRET: Nar me no go up dem stairs.

DOLE: Cha even his own man a left him.

ZIPPY: Cha, him get wise.

MARCUS: Hey Mister Zippy you fer want ter go me no yer need one excuse ter need she.

ZIPPY: Excuse me ras, you a look in mirror ter ras.

MARCUS: All right me going, me en want see she ras but she come fer dis.

MARCUS *goes upstairs.*

DOLE: Cha.

ZIPPY: Dat ras cha make me a take a walk round de corner.

DOLE: Yer do' want for stay.

ZIPPY: Cha wat for him (*Going to the door.*) a go just come down wit him ras, talk.

DOLE: Yer a come Fret.

FRET: Yea.

They all leave.

Act Two

The centre.
MARCUS's *board in a prominent position.*
A large football on top.
MARCUS *is at the Juke Box dancing.*

ZIPPY, DOLE *and* FRET *run in.*

MARCUS: Cha, whey all yer a go. Me taught all a get lock up.

DOLE: We was up de road.

FRET *pulls out a pair of jeans from under his robe.*

MARCUS: Cha. Jeans a hippy ting. Wha happening up dey?

DOLE: Notting much. Some chick a walk about.

MARCUS: Any a no?

DOLE: Julie en she friend.

MARCUS: Cha dem a make some style.

DOLE: Dem say dem was coming down, but wen dem hear you was here dem change dem mind.

MARCUS: Cha yer ras clart mouth lie.

DOLE: It a true dem say you a too weird dem say you a favour Frankenstein monster, ter ras clart.

MARCUS: Tell dem me a favour Casanova ter ras, me d' want dem me have me own chick.

DOLE: Yer a pull a new chick?

MARCUS: Yes nar.

DOLE: Who?

MARCUS: De new chick wat she name Gail.

DOLE: You pull she?

MARCUS: Cha, wha so hard in dat? It was a easy, me do' let dem night class chick frighten me. Dem brains do' distract me, me cope wid all a dem have ter trew at me.

DOLE: Yer hear dat Zippy?

ZIPPY: Me hear, what dat have ter do wit me? Dat him ras clart business wat him do.

DOLE: Whey she is?

MARCUS: You want it, it a upstairs resting.

DOLE: It good?

MARCUS: Cha it en bad me make it good.

DOLE: Cha man yer a quick ter ras.

MARCUS: Cha me give she me power, me make she tink me is wise man, an she car keep no secret from me. Me make she believe me no everyting bout she dat me no all she dark secret, an make she a beg me tell she how me no. But wat she en a no is me a read she application letter to Sandy an me no all bout she, she believe me have power man, wisdom ter ras clart me is she savior ter ras.

DOLE: Cha you is champion now.

MARCUS: Cha, who want one game? Me feeling strong.

MARCUS *punches the juke box.*

DOLE: Me play yer ter ras.

DOLE *goes to the game. They play.* SANDY *and* JACKO *enter.*

SANDY: Well I see everything's still normal, football and noise. How's everything?

DOLE: All right. Cha.

SANDY: Zippy?

ZIPPY: All right.

SANDY: Fret?

FRET: Easy.

SANDY: Good then. How's Gail?

MARCUS: She a O.K., take me word for it.

He laughs.

SANDY: Yes?

DOLE: Him no.

SANDY: I see. Well Marcus, Jacko wants a return match.

MARCUS: Cha me beat him ras already. Look pon wall we put up me award. Me is champion.

SANDY: Go on, give him a game.

MARCUS: Cha all right make me finish beat Dole first.

SANDY: All right I'll just go and see how Gail is coping.

MARCUS: Cha she coping fine.

SANDY: That's what I'm worried about.

SANDY *goes.* JACKO *sits next to* ZIPPY.

ZIPPY: So how yer fine tings, it change?

JACKO: A bit a just have ter get use ter some new . . .

SANDY *brings* GAIL *downstairs.* GAIL's *face is bloodied.*

SANDY: For christ sake Marcus what did you do this for?

MARCUS: Me no do notting.

JACKO: Wat happen?

SANDY: Marcus you did this. Why for christ sake did you hit the girl? You had no right to.

MARCUS: Me no hit she.

SANDY: She said you did, look at her, why should she lie?

GAIL: He hit me, he came.

MARCUS: Me no hit you you fall down, me no hit she she a fall down, me try an pick she up.

SANDY: Shut up for christ sake, shut up. What happened Gail?

GAIL: He came upstairs, and started to play his game and tried to get me going putting me in a corner, and wanting to touch me and putting his hands . . .

SANDY: Did he . . . No O.K. all right O.K., all right, all right, don't cry, don't . . .

MARCUS: Me never touch she.

SANDY: You're a wicked, dirty, vicious bastard that's what you are, I always knew one day . . .

MARCUS: Wat?

A beat.

Go en take she word for it, just because she's a woman, an better educated you tink dem people do' lie.

SANDY: Wat's that got to do with it? Look at her. (*A beat.*) Zippy go upstairs and get the First Aid Box you know where it is.

ZIPPY: Yea. (*He runs upstairs.*)

DOLE: So Marcus you a pull she eh, you a one focking mad ras clart.

MARCUS: Me no try a touch she, me box she ras clart. She a tink cause she a educated she a better dan me, but me have 'O' levels just like she, me do' show off da is all an try an talk like de English Man, and beg him for job in him office. She a black just like me how come she get a job in dis place? She no better, me proud just like she, cha she a ras clart hypocrite black woman.

ZIPPY *returns with the box.*

SANDY (*takes the box*): Thanks.

She takes out cotton wool and a small bottle.

This won't sting. I'll just clean off the blood. There, there, how does that feel, is that better?

GAIL: Yes – Sandy he –

SANDY: Don't worry it's all right.

GAIL: He's a liar.

SANDY: Yes, yes I know.

MARCUS: Dats right believe she, me no you like woman, you always take woman side in tings.

SANDY: What do you mean by that?

MARCUS: Me no you do' like man, all dem young girl who come here you always nice ter dem always want ter touch dem an get dem ter like you, but dem do' come no more dem no yer dem no yer secret, yer do see dem no come.

SANDY: Marcus, you're nasty and dirty and vicious, they don't come because you frighten them away, they know you better than I did. I – I – now go away and take your dirty mind with you.

MARCUS *moves. He sits.*
The boys go to the football game and play.

(*To* GAIL): What do you want to do now? Do you want to go home?

GAIL: No, I want to go to the Police Station.

SANDY: What?

GAIL: I want to report it.

SANDY: Gail, you don't . . .

GAIL: I want to report that nasty vicious thing. I want to report what he did to me.

SANDY: You don't know what will happen.

GAIL: It will show him. He's got to realise he cannot hit a woman, an get away with it.

She gets up.

SANDY: Gail, Please – (*She sits her down.*) If you go to the Police you know what they'll do? They will come here and take him away, he's already on suspended sentences. He'll go in for sure and what will that prove?

GAIL: It will show him he can't treat people like this and get away with it.

SANDY: He's an animal that's what he is that's how he's been made, that's how he's been treated.

GAIL: Sandy, you . . .

SANDY: I know he's a liar, and vicious. What did you think you were doing when you came here? Did you think you were coming to a kindergarten? These boys are all vicious, not as bad as Marcus but, that's why they're here, that's why society pays us, to keep them away from good clean society, out of trouble, out of prison. That's why this place is open. You know how I had to fight to get you here? If you go to the Police, they'll close us down. We're meant to be qualified to do it, to do their dirty work for them.

GAIL: Sandy.

SANDY: Jacko, you tell her, tell her what it's like . . . tell her what will happen if he goes in.

JACKO: I en involved in dis, I en no what happening.

SANDY: Can't you see what's happened?

JACKO: I en no, I en no.

SANDY: You want him to go inside, you want him to go through what you went through?

JACKO: Why yer asking me? I do' no, me en no judge or jury, do' ask me.

SANDY: Well I'm asking you Gail, I'm begging you. I'll ban him from here. I'll do anything, but don't report him. Believe me that's the worst.

GAIL: I'm going.

She goes to leave.

SANDY: Gail, I know Marcus lied, you think I don't? I know what he's like, you think I haven't been jammed in a corner before and had hands all over me? But when I looked in their eyes they were as puzzled as I was and as frightened. They do it, they don't even know why they . . .

GAIL: He hit me, Sandy he . . .

SANDY: I was just like you when I started here full of bright ideas. I was going to make it happen. I knew exactly what was needed, but there is a world outside that I can't change. They haven't got a chance the moment they walk on the street they're guilty, that's why we're here to occupy them, to contain them because society doesn't want to know, not even their parents . . .

JACKO: Dat en true.

SANDY: You went inside right?

JACKO: Yes.

SANDY: Did your Mother visit you?

JACKO: No.

SANDY: Did any of your family visit?

JACKO: No.

SANDY: You told me how nice it would be if your father came. I have the letters to prove . . .

JACKO: Dat was foolishness. I was too soft. I believe in your fairy story.

SANDY (*to* GAIL): Yes, I let them dress up an fool around and dream about Africa. What else is there? That's all they've got.

JACKO: All dat is foolishness too. Ethiopia is a Marxist country an Haile Selassie is dead an he exploit he own people more dan anybody. Dat en true blackness, blackness is seeing tings de way it is nothing more. Inside, inside prison. I was in prison, but me en no whey all yer was. I read all de time I in dey, everyting, I read about how de National Front an dem terrorising black people an nobody en doing notting, an how dis Rastaman ting saying peace and love an smoking dope an dreaming bout Africa an de Bible, an de National Front attacking people. I car understand all yer. Wha happen, all yer car see, all yer blind? I say wen I come out I go meet de Youth fighting back, because de paper en go print dem ting, an I go join dem. But de paper right. Wen I went in people eye was opening, now I come out it close. Wha happen, wha happen ter all yer? We fight de racist in prison. All yer outside, wha all yer do?

MARCUS: What all yer listen ter he for? He en no genuine black man.

JACKO *approaches* MARCUS.

JACKO: So you're going to Ethiopia den?

MARCUS: Sure.

JACKO: What you going ter to do wen you get dere?

MARCUS: Me go do my ting. (*He backs off.*)

JACKO: So you believe in peace an love, eh?

MARCUS: Yes, dat's what de Bible good book say.

JACKO: You love me? (*He pushes MARCUS.*)

MARCUS: Me do' want no . . .

JACKO: Give me some peace and love.

MARCUS: Me do' want no fight man, Sandy, tell him.

SANDY: Jacko . . .

MARCUS: Sandy, tell him. (*He pulls out a blade.*)

SANDY: Marcus, don't.

JACKO: Where your peace an love? Give me a kiss you black bastard.

MARCUS: Me warn you.

He lunges at JACKO. JACKO *overpowers* MARCUS, *grabs the knife and holds it against his throat. Then he lets* MARCUS *go.*

SANDY: Oh my god.

MARCUS runs out. Music. ZIPPY *walks out. They all follow* ZIPPY, *one by one, leaving* SANDY *alone on stage.*